MARVEL STUDIOS

THE INFINITY SAGA

THOR RAGNAROK

WRITTEN BY
ELENI ROUSSOS

FOREWORD BY
TAIKA WAITITI

AFTERWORD AND DUSTJACKET ART BY
ANDY PARK

COVER ART BY
FRANCISCO RUIZ AFTER JACK KIRBY

BOOK DESIGN BY
ADAM DEL RE

PROJECT MANAGER
ALEX SCHARF

THOR CREATED BY
STAN LEE, LARRY LIEBER AND JACK KIRBY

TITAN BOOKS

FOR MARVEL PUBLISHING
JEFF YOUNGQUIST, Editor
SARAH SINGER, Editor, Special Projects
JEREMY WEST, Manager, Licensed Publishing
SVEN LARSEN, VP, Licensed Publishing
DAVID GABRIEL, VP, Print & Digital Publishing
C.B. CEBULSKI, Editor in Chief

FOR MARVEL STUDIOS 2017
KEVIN FEIGE, President
LOUIS D'ESPOSITO, Co-President
VICTORIA ALONSO, Executive Vice President, Visual Effects
BRAD WINDERBAUM, Vice President, Production & Development
BRIAN CHAPEK, Production & Development Executive
WILL CORONA PILGRIM, Creative Director, Research & Development
RYAN POTTER, VP Business Affairs
ERIKA DENTON, Clearances Director
RANDY McGOWAN, VP Technical Operations
AXEL SCHARF, Production Asset Manager
DAVID GRANT, Vice President, Physical Production
ALEXIS AUDITORE, Manager, Physical Assets

MARVEL STUDIOS' THE INFINITY SAGA - THOR: RAGNAROK - THE ART OF THE MOVIE

ISBN: 9781803368504

First edition: November 2025

10 9 8 7 6 5 4 3 2 1

Published by Titan Books
A division of Titan Publishing Group Ltd
144 Southwark St, London SE1 0UP

www.titanbooks.com

EU RP (for authorities only)
eucomply OÜ Pärnu mnt 139b-14 11317
Talinn, Estonia
hello@eucompliancepartner.com
+3375690241

Did you enjoy this book? We love to hear from our readers. Please e-mail us at: readerfeedback@titanemail.com or write to Reader Feedback at the above address.

To receive advance information, news, competitions, and exclusive offers online, please sign up for the Titan newsletter on our website: www.titanbooks.com

A CIP catalogue record for this title is available from the British Library.

Printed in China

■ RUIZ AFTER KIRBY, 2-3 SZE SZE ▶

THOR: RAGNAROK

THE ART OF

»PRESS START«

TCSS

FOREWORD 2017

by TAIKA WAITITI

Hello.

This book contains art from the movie *Thor: Ragnarok*. If this is not the book you were looking for, please close it and back away. Slowly. The art and designs contained within these pages are dangerous, bold, groundbreaking, tumultuous, crazy, delicious, and should be approached with care and wide-eyed curiosity. And gloves.

Firstly I'd like to acknowledge Andy Park and the other amazing artists in Marvel's Visual Development team. Without people like Andy and Ryan Meinerding, this book wouldn't exist. It's through their astounding character design and development that the MCU looks so good. Even before I joined this journey, they had been painting concepts for characters and scenes that have been touchstones for us throughout the entire process.

Our Production Design team, headed by Dan Hennah and Ra Vincent, performed impossible feats on a daily basis, creating an inordinate amount of props and sets, all meticulously crafted to perfection. Seeing it all come to life was an incredible experience. Often I would doodle away on a sketch pad, hand a couple of drawings to the guys, and stumble onto set a few months later to find they had turned my crappy scribble into a spaceship or laser gun.

You'll also see a lot of concepts for characters and their costumes designed by the great Mayes C. Rubeo, who is an artist and champion of her craft. Seeing her designs come to life gave me endless joy. You'll also see some of the incredible storyboards that were created very early on in the process. I'm always amazed by these artists' ability to capture dynamic action from a film that doesn't yet exist, and if you watch the movie while holding this book in front of you, you'll see images that we've copied directly from their boards. They're that good.

I'd also like to name-drop one very important person: Jack Kirby. From the beginning, I had wanted to incorporate Kirby's style into the design of the film. There had been hints at it in the other Marvel movies, but not to the extent that we were planning. We eventually told ourselves, "If we're going to do this, let's do it properly and run headfirst into the Kirbyfication of our film." This meant throwing ourselves at the feet of the King and allowing ourselves to unapologetically lift (steal) his designs and take them for our own. We pushed our team to use his work as inspiration, reminding them that in the case of Kirby, more is more.

We focused most of this energy into the design of the gladiatorial planet of Sakaar. A dumping ground for all lost things in the universe, Sakaar is a lawless world made up of junk that is repurposed again and again until it finds value and meaning. It's the kind of place where doomed space travelers discover their fate is either as a gladiatorial fighter...or food. A world ruled by a twisted lunatic called the Grandmaster, Sakaar is the one place in the Marvel Universe where Kirby's art makes perfect sense.

It feels amazing to have been a part of this process, and it isn't until seeing all of the art collected in this book that one realizes just how much work goes into these productions. I come from the lonely world of indie filmmaking, where you do most of the work yourself. However, at Marvel, there are countless artists, way more talented than I, who give their very best ideas so directors can look like they know what they're doing. I am immensely grateful to the artists and design teams involved in the making of this film for their tireless work and the creation of truly mind-blowing concepts—all of which I will be taking credit for.

Lastly, I'd like to thank the producers—Kevin Feige, Lou D'Eposito, Victoria Alonso, and Brad Winderbaum—for taking a chance on a young, good-looking, renegade filmmaker from New Zealand, and inviting him to join the coolest gang in town.

■ PREVIOUS THE THIRD FLOOR, INC

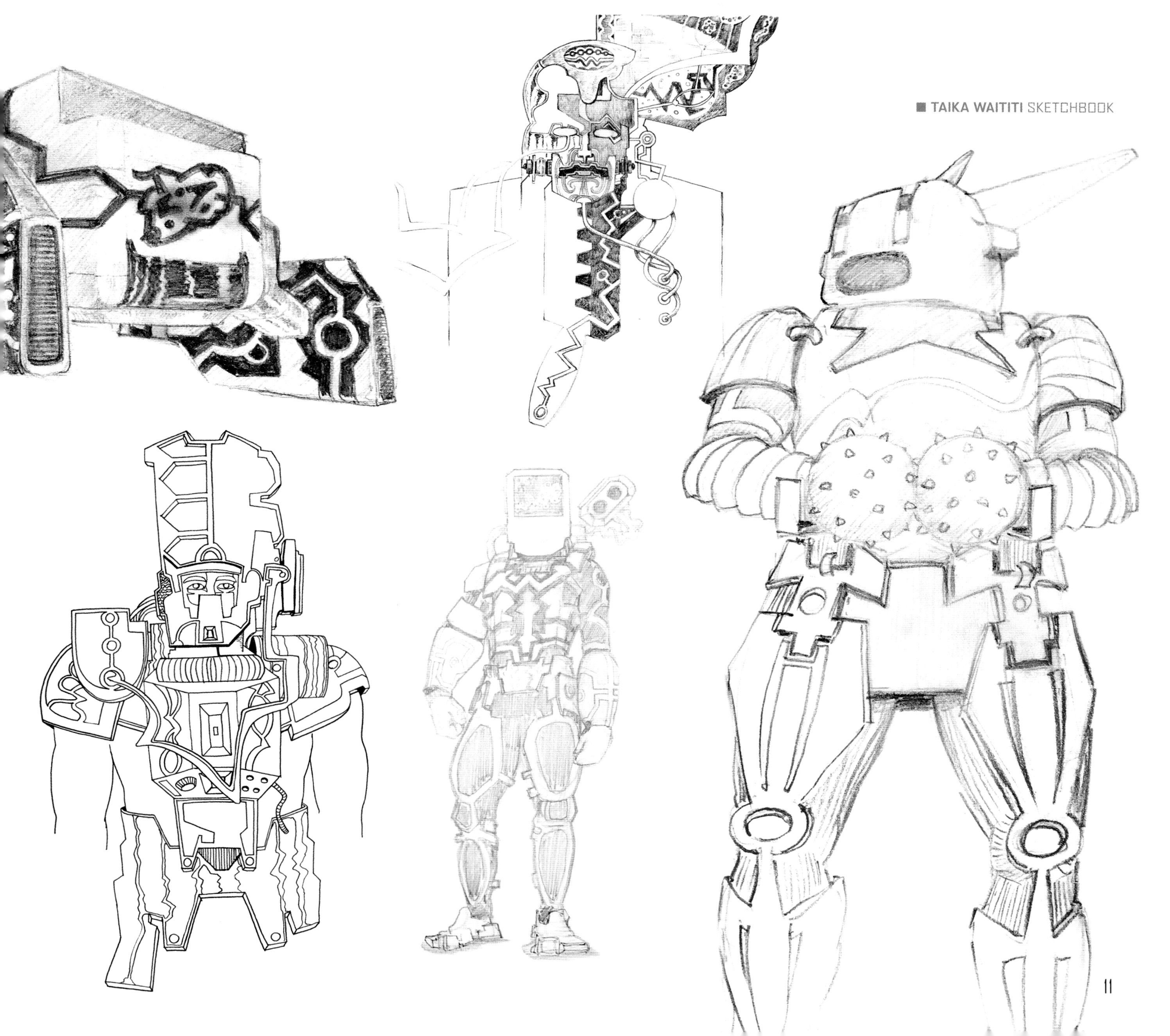

INTRODUCTION

The world of Thor Odinson has changed dramatically since his first appearance in the Marvel Cinematic Universe. Long gone are the days of rebellious adventures with Lady Sif and the Warriors Three. After Loki's betrayal, long gone are the moments of brother trusting brother. There is no longer peace in the universe, and something dangerous is looming on the horizon.

"The last time we saw Thor, he had just fought an army of robots on Earth, and he knows more than the other Avengers," Executive Producer Brad Winderbaum says. "He's privy to the world of the gods. He knows that Infinity Stones are starting to pop up. And he knows that somebody gave his brother the scepter that has caused two *Avengers* movies' worth of havoc on Earth. And now he's going to go back up into the stars and figure out where these things came from. In investigating that, he soon uncovers a much bigger, more sinister, more terrible conspiracy that has been happening for as long as Thor has been a hero in the Marvel Universe.

"It's a universal threat that's a game changer for the MCU. So much in the way that *Captain America: The Winter Soldier* saw the fall of S.H.I.E.L.D., which laid the foundation for *Avengers: Age of Ultron* and the MCU moving forward, *Thor: Ragnarok* will set up the universe in a similar way and create a scenario where nothing is the same again."

To understand how this film is destined to further shake up Marvel's cinematic landscape, one simply need look at the sequel's titular event, Ragnarok.

When they created the character of Thor in 1962, Stan Lee, Larry Lieber, and Jack Kirby sought inspiration in Norse mythology. Filled with characters including Odin, Heimdall, and Loki—and grand halls such as Valhalla and Asgard—the myths of the Vikings included tales of Ragnarök, the fate of the gods.

A tale believed to have been passed down by bards and minstrels until finally being written down in the 13th century A.D., the Skaldic poem *Völuspá* from *The Poetic Edda* tells the story of a prophetess describing the creation of the world, its impending doom, and eventual rebirth. The poem's climax details the events of Ragnarök—the death of the gods and the end of the world.

"Ragnarök is the Norse concept of the apocalypse, the end of days, Armageddon, and really what we're exploring with this idea of Ragnarok is that Asgard is under threat," Director Taika Waititi says. "And definitely in the Asgardian culture, they believe it's the end of Asgard. It's the death of many of the heroes that we have come to love."

While the end of Asgard as we know it is a serious subject matter, the filmmakers still wanted to have fun with the characters and take them in new and exciting directions.

◄▲▼ BEFORE PRODUCTION BEGAN ON *THOR: RAGNAROK*, **DIRECTOR TAIKA WAITITI** CREATED A SHORT PIECE TO TEASE THE FILM: TEAM THOR. NOT ONLY DID WAITITI DIRECT, BUT HE WAS ALSO ABLE TO STRETCH HIS ARTISTIC MUSCLES, HELPING CREATE ARTWORK FOR THE PROJECT. THE FINAL CUT WAS SHOWN AT SAN DIEGO COMIC CON 2016, AND WAS INCLUDED ON THE BLU-RAY AND DIGITAL DOWNLOAD FOR *CAPTAIN AMERICA: CIVIL WAR*.

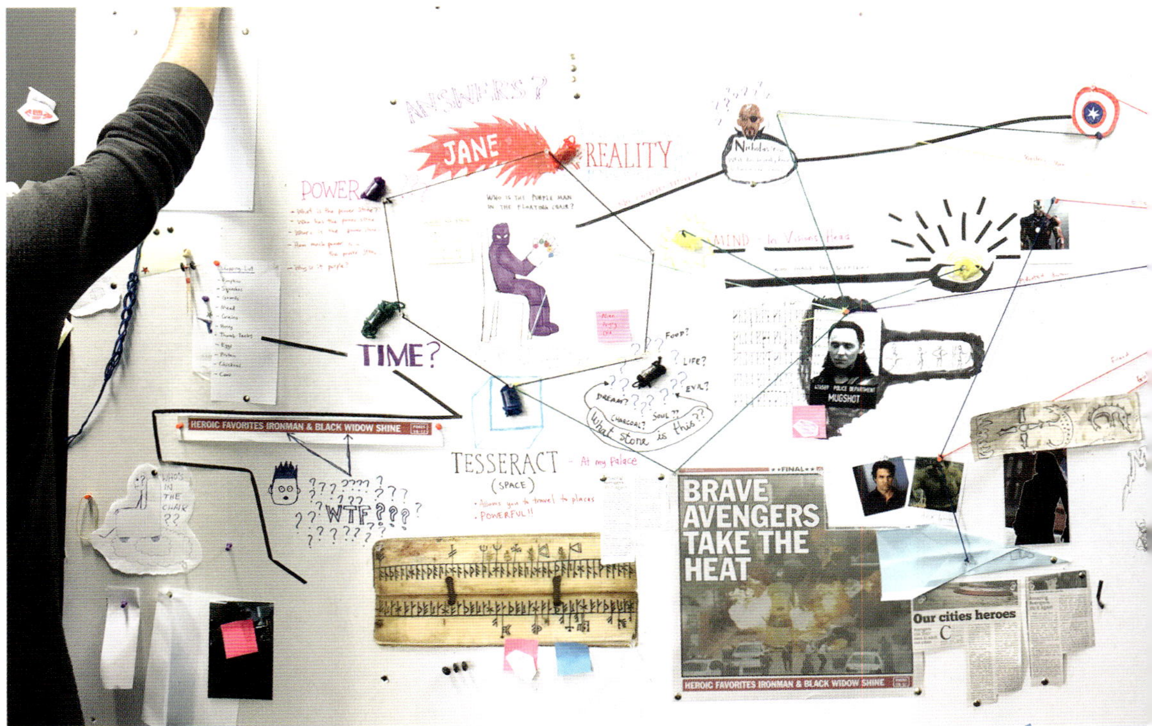

▲ SIMONSON & OLYOPTICS 2.0

KIRBY & COLLETTA ►

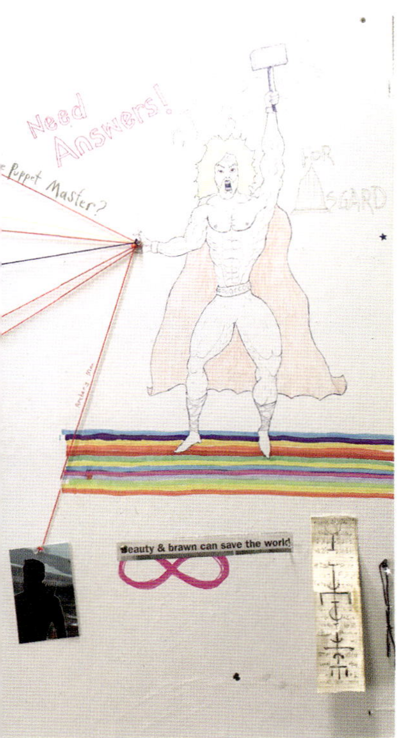

President of Marvel Studios and Executive Producer Kevin Feige recalls the team's preliminary discussions regarding early story explorations. "We were talking about how to bring Thor's next adventure to life. There's so much to explore between Thor and Loki with Odin involved. We left Thor and Loki on a bit of a cliffhanger in the last film. Loki's now ruling Asgard—he's taken on the guise of Odin—so certainly we wanted to explore that and see where that would take us. But it was very important to us, like we had done with *The Winter Soldier* and *Ant-Man*: How do we take Thor and bring him to a new genre? Science fiction and the tradition of the very serious Norse mythology served us very well in his early films. But this time, how do we take him to another place? How do we take him to another side of the universe and have more fun with it? Keep those stakes real, keep the mythological storylines true and accurate, but at the same time have a lot more fun with Thor."

Responsible for launching Thor in that bold new direction is Waititi. "Marvel has a great tradition of hiring really exciting filmmakers who can bring new life into these super hero movies," Winderbaum says. "What we love is when a filmmaker comes in and has a very specific vision for what new kind of genre sandbox a film can take place in. We've had Jon Favreau taking Iron Man and turning it into a James Bond-style techno thriller, Joss Whedon bringing the ensemble together for *The Avengers*, James Gunn creating the '80s pop version of *Guardians of the Galaxy*, the Russo brothers creating a 1970s-style espionage film out of *Captain America*, and Peyton Reed creating a comedic heist film out of *Ant-Man*. We're always looking for that new voice that's going to bring something unexpected into the limitless sphere of super heroes.

"When Taika came in and pitched a kind of cosmic space race, rock-opera, or heavy-metal version of Thor, we were in. Something that Taika does, which we really value at Marvel, is create a real sense of pathos with the characters. You really understand what these people are up against, and even when it's funny and humorous you feel like the stakes are really true for these people."

The filmmakers also were ready to change up the visual style for Thor's next adventure. While writer/artist Walter Simonson's run on the Thor comic book from 1983-1984 heavily inspired the storyline for *Thor: Ragnarok*, the film's designers and artists analyzed the legendary Jack Kirby's work for ways in which to incorporate his visual style.

Kirby was an innovator in the medium. His illustrations have a unique form and design—expressive compositions with hard, exaggerated lines and dynamic shapes. His technique for depicting various forms of energy—the Kirby Krackle—has become an industry standard.

"Jack Kirby is a big part of this film, in the design of a lot of the Sakaaran work that we're creating," Waititi says. "He's a huge hero for all of us. And if you look around at all the offices, you'll see this beautiful Kirby art. We've been influenced a lot by all of his art for the design of our spaceships and the patterning, and our costumes. All the departments are taking that on board and paying great homage to Kirby with what we're doing in this film.

"I feel so lucky to be able to bring his legacy to the big screen. It's been a long time, and we finally are able to show the world what a genius he was. His line, his color, everything—we're trying to embrace that and bring that into this film."

"I was very familiar with Jack Kirby from my childhood reading comics in the '60s, so I knew who he was," Production Designer Dan Hennah says. "And when his name came up, Taika, Kevin, and Brad all embraced the idea that this new world, Sakaar, should be a Kirby world. There's so many ways you can go with a design aesthetic; when that was chosen and agreed on, and everyone felt that this is where we should go, then it was a really easy thing to embrace. And then say, 'Okay, how far can we take it? What can we do with it?'"

In addition to influencing style and design in comics, Kirby is responsible for helping create dozens of beloved Marvel characters—including Captain America, Iron Man, Thor, the Hulk, the Fantastic Four, and the X-Men. Several classic villains also make the list, including *Thor: Ragnarok's* main antagonist, Hela.

The Goddess of Death, Hela has long been a fan-favorite. First appearing in 1964's *Journey Into Mystery #102*, she has frequently visited chaos, death, and destruction upon the Nine Realms.

"We're introducing what we think is one of the most iconic villains in the history of Marvel comics, Hela, who in our film will be the first female villain that we've had," Feige says. "She is unbelievable. She is as scary and deadly and charming as any villain we've ever had. And when you have a film with Loki in it, if you're going to have another villain, she better be charming. She better be charismatic. She better be scary. Because she's going have to top him. And Loki arguably is our best villain to date. Hela needs to surpass that."

"Hela is going to be a badass," Winderbaum says. "She's going to be like nothing else we've had before in the universe. We want her to be fun and infectious in a way and exciting and dangerous to watch. She's a character you want to see more of on-screen,

■ KIRBY & COLLETTA

◄ LEFT **YU & MCCAIG**
RIGHT **ROMITA**

▲ **PAGULAYAN, HUET & SOTOMAYOR**

who's so charismatic, but at the same time you're afraid of what she's going to do next."

"She's not only strong and beautiful, but she's also funny," Waititi says. "And she's flawed. And she has layers. And she's tormented. And she's got a lot more going on than I think some of the more typical villains that you see in these kinds of films. She's not just about taking over the world, or owning the universe, which you see so much now. She wants something that I think a lot of people can kind of relate to: She wants to come back home and be accepted, and she wants what's hers."

And to get that, she'll have to go through not only Thor, but also someone else who's pretty incredible. "What's always fun—I've said this for years, and all of us at Marvel Studios know this—is that the comics were so amazing, having this shared universe where anybody could've shown up in anybody else's books," Feige says. "And certainly we've done that with the Avengers films. We saw the Falcon show up in *Ant-Man*. We even saw Captain America show up ever so briefly in *Thor: The Dark World*. Spider-Man showed up in *Captain America: Civil War*. So it did seem like, how do we take two of our biggest, most powerful characters and do that classic team-up? With Thor and with Hulk and with Hulk's history in the comics, he felt like the perfect choice to bring into that Thor world."

Hulk is no stranger to cosmic adventures. In the epic "Planet Hulk" storyline—serialized from 2006-2007 in *Incredible Hulk #92-105*—Hulk is betrayed and exiled into space by Earth's heroes, landing on Sakaar. Sold into slavery, Hulk becomes the Green Scar, the planet's mightiest gladiator—eventually leading a rebellion against the tyrannical Red King. The filmmakers borrowed elements from writer Greg Pak's fan-favorite, critically acclaimed story to inspire their own versions of the gladiatorial tournaments and Sakaar.

"[Hulk] goes into a wormhole, and he ends up on this planet Sakaar," says actor Mark Ruffalo, who portrays Bruce Banner. "It follows in the comic that Hulk has become this champion of this planet as a gladiator. He doesn't turn into Banner anymore because he's always fighting and raging.

"I think we get into it deeper. We have to explain that a little bit more, so we do that in this movie. Thor basically ends up [on Sakaar] by accident, and he just happens to run into Hulk. [Thor's] going have to fight in the gladiator stadium against the champion, and when the champion comes out he realizes he's fighting Hulk; it's good luck for him because he needs Hulk at this moment in time to save his planet, Asgard. Thor has got to finally go back and claim the throne, and he needs Hulk to help him to do that."

Some other new faces also will be joining in the fight for Asgard, along with some old favorites. With so many new and exciting characters, a genre switch-up, and new planets and realms to explore, there's so much for audiences to enjoy. Screenwriter Eric Pearson, however, has one simple wish for viewers of the film. "I just hope that they leave with a lot of conflicting favorite parts and characters. I feel like we've done a lot of new things in here. I want them to be arguing about what the best part was."

THE SIGNS OF
RAGNAROK

The sun turns pale;
The spacious earth
The sea engulphs;
From heaven fall
The lucid stars:
At the end of time,
The vapours rage,
And playful flames
Involve the skies.

- Excerpt from *The Poetic Edda* as translated by Ebenezer Henderson (1819)

Two years have passed since Thor said goodbye to Earth and the Avengers. Having seen a vision in the Water of Sight during *Avengers: Age of Ultron*, he has traveled back to the cosmos in search of answers regarding the continued emergence of Infinity Stones and the identity of the mastermind behind this threat. While searching for the answer, he is continually plagued by terrible dreams, all pointing to the fact that Ragnarok is drawing near.

Road-weary but determined, Thor learns that Surtur, the fire giant, is wreaking havoc on the Nine Realms. Diverting from his original quest, the God of Thunder travels to the fire realm of Muspelheim and becomes a willing prisoner in order to gain the information he needs to stop him.

"So the last time we'd seen Thor on screen was in *Avengers: Age of Ultron*," Chris Hemsworth says. "And he basically is sort of off to search deeper into the villain who seems to be orchestrating all of the problems that are affecting all of the characters in the Marvel Universe. But we don't really get bogged down with a lot of that sort of backstory.

"We make this, I think, a fairly unique film. At the beginning, we find Thor in a bit of a journey of self-discovery. He's from Asgard, but turned down being king and lived on Earth—but still he's not from Earth, so he doesn't quite fit in there. So he's off searching for answers. On his way, he discovers things that have been unleashed and villains that are causing all sorts of chaos."

◄ **SZE**
PREVIOUS **BEN-MIMOUN** WITH **DEL RE**

THOR

Whenever filmmakers bring a previously established MCU character back to the big screen, they try to come up with new and interesting ways to depict the character—and the Odinson is no exception. The team made sure that from the start, Thor's fifth onscreen appearance would provide clues about what he's been doing since *Avengers: Age of Ultron.*

"Taika had a conversation with me about making him the road-worn Thor," Visual Development Supervisor Andy Park says. "He told me Thor had been on a two-year journey and had not changed since he started. He doesn't care what he looks like because he is so determined, and he just refused to put his hammer down and change instantly, because he can do that. He's just too busy. So he became dirtier with a longer beard. He's not all glammed out in his blingy Asgardian look. He's a bit more rugged."

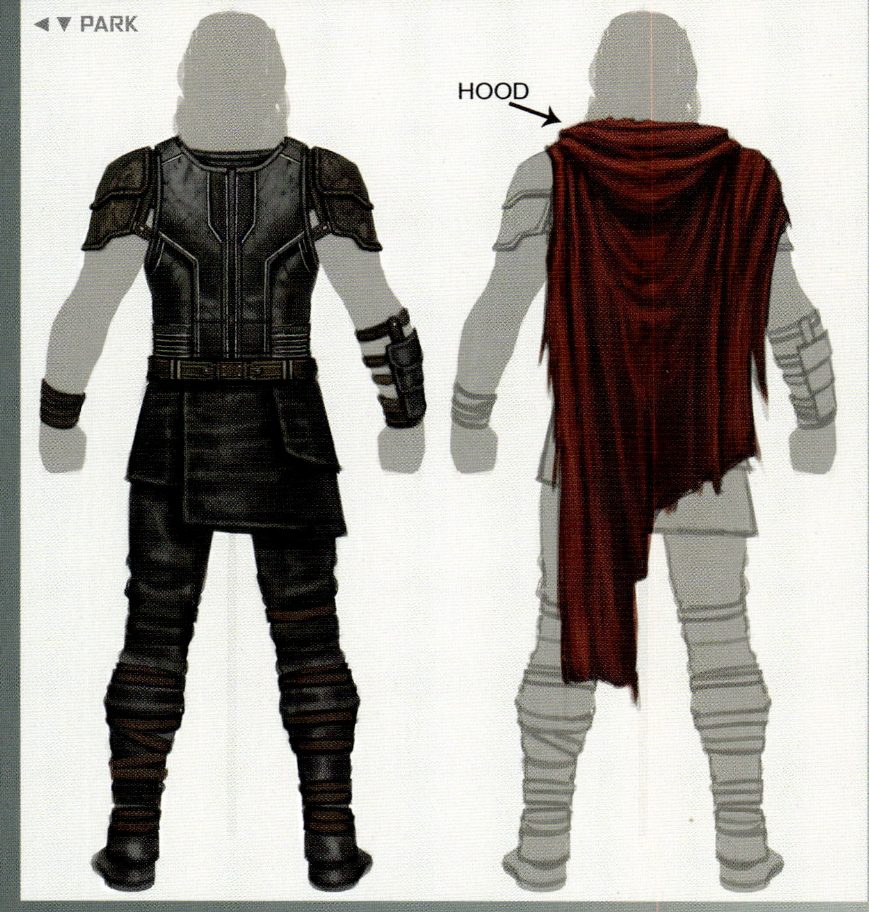

◄ ▼ PARK

■ PARK

▲SZE

FRANCISCO ▶

▲ REES

▲ REES

▲ **BEN-MIMOUN**

ALLAN ▶

"I think that what we do as a job—making films and telling stories in this medium, getting to build incredible sets like this, dressing up in these crazy outfits, and creating stories and adventures and entertainment—shouldn't feel like hard work," Director Taika Waititi says. "It is hard work. It's very hard work. And it's one of the hardest things that I've ever done in my life. But I don't think you should ever really come to work feeling like, 'Oh, man, I've got to go to work.' I want people to come to work excited. It's a new day, new opportunities. We're going to discover new things, and the way that I work is that I think the script is a kind of a suggestion. We will often rewrite stuff on the day, which we did for most of the film. And we improvise a lot."

24-25 **ALLAN**, 26-27 **REES**

SURTUR

The fire giant Surtur has been giving Thor hell since 1963's *Journey Into Mystery #97*, and now the fire demon gets his chance to wreak havoc on the big screen thanks to a talented team of designers and visual-effects artists. "It's starting with a charcoal black skeleton, and then you start wrapping layers of muscle," says Visual Effects Supervisor Jake Morrison. "Imagine all the scary textbooks that you read in biology, and you saw all the muscle lines that ran down. Instead of that being flesh, it's plasma down those groups of muscles. And then you put a layer of liquid fire on top of that, almost like a lava suspension. Next, you put this sort of crusty, hard, dried lava level over the top that. And then, as he moves, none of that can stretch—it all has to float on top like a second skin. It actually ends up making him look slightly scabrous, which is kind of cool. It adds to the villain kind of aspect of the whole thing. He's a lot of fun to work with and is a really visually complex creature."

▲ HEMPSON

BRICLOT ▶

BRICLOT

■ BRICLOT

THOR3
DEAD BONES
SURTUR
muspelheim
fire
old
primeval culture

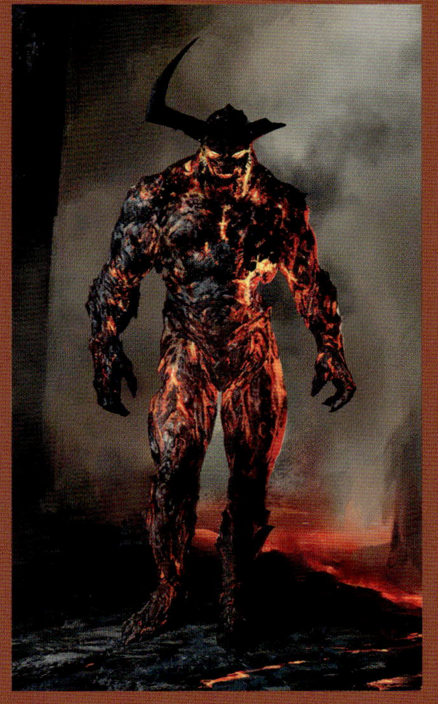

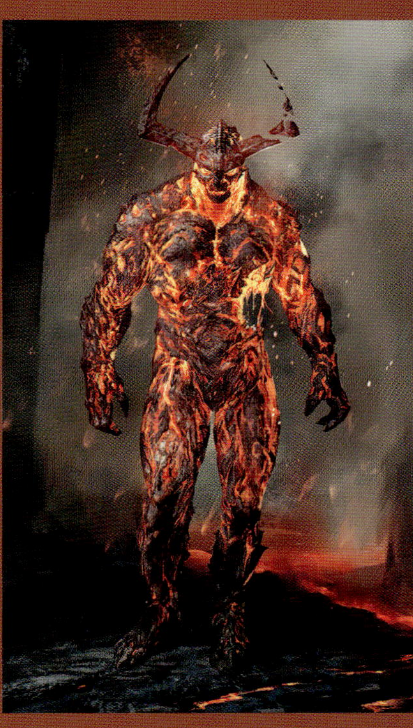

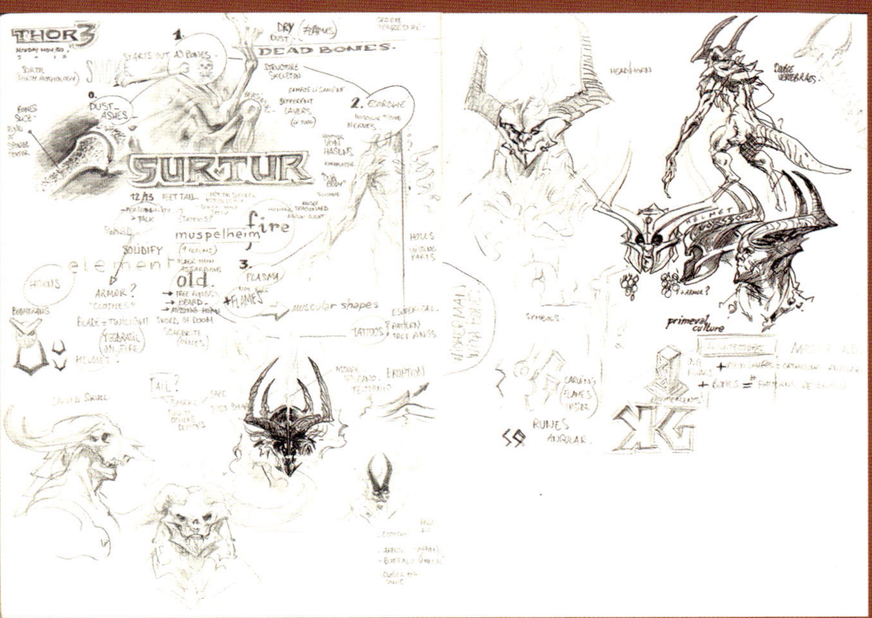

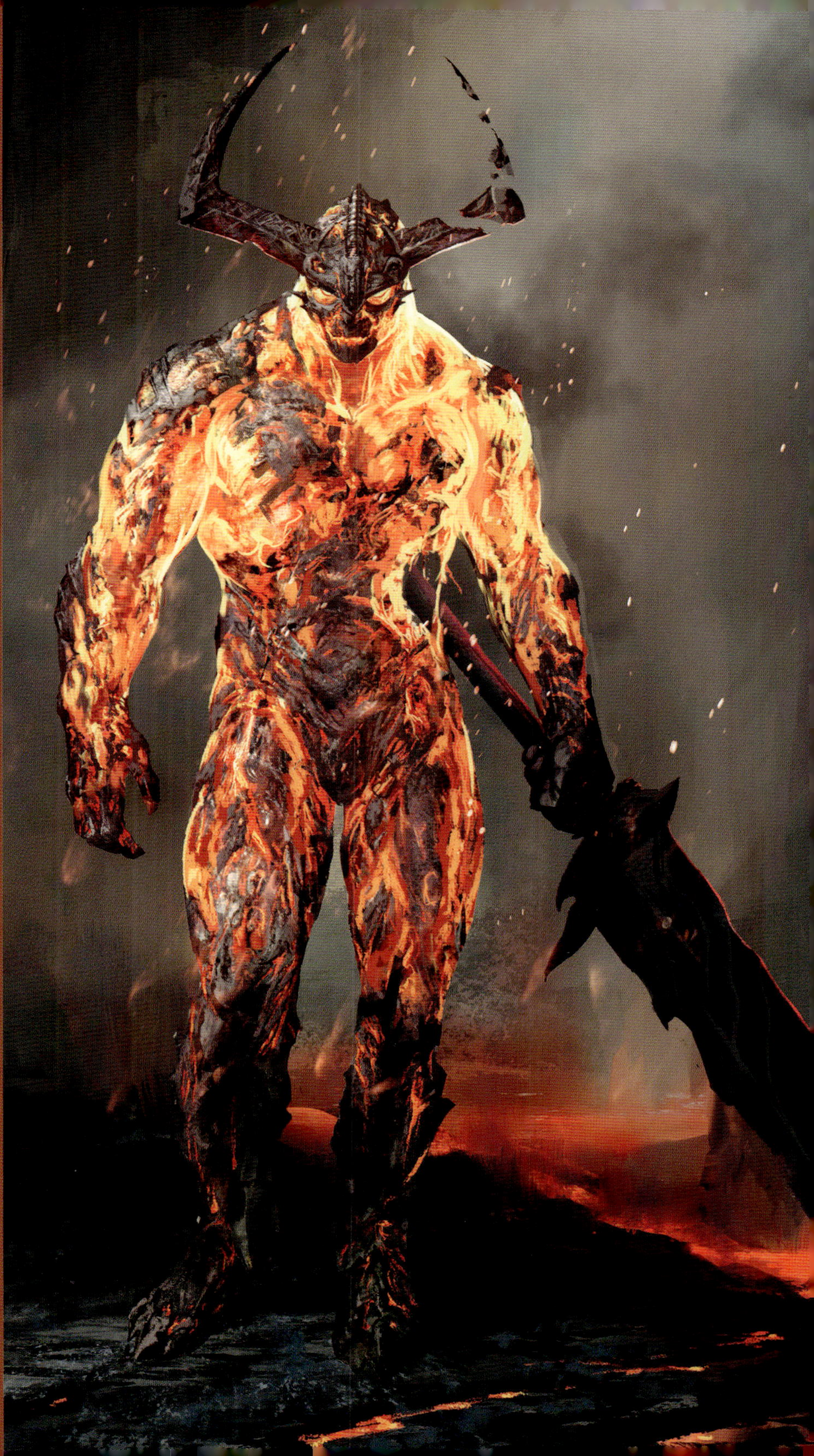

■ BRICLOT

■ SZE

■ FRANCISCO

BRICLOT

"These are probably the earliest designs I did for *Thor: Ragnarok*," Concept Artist Jackson Sze says. "Surtur was the character they wanted to see some iterations for first. The idea of a flaming-skeleton monster is not entirely novel in the entertainment industry, so I was just trying to find some way to make it a little bit different—either through ornate armor or magma-lava type of textures."

◄ **BRICLOT** ■ **SZE**

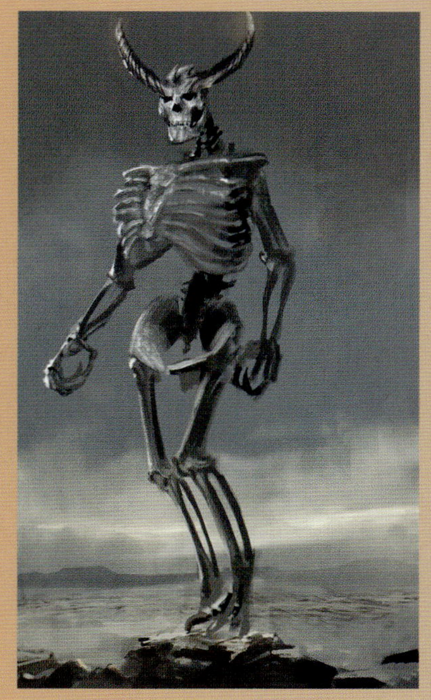

◄ KUTSCHE

■ ORTIZ

Helping the fire giant in his altercation with Thor are thousands of fire demons. Eager to serve their king, they swarm Thor, poised to attack. "The main idea is that they were a kind of living lava, cracked and kind of broken, but not too sympathetic," Concept Artist Ian Joyner says. "Some of the earlier versions I had done looked a little too cute and were something you wouldn't really want to see Thor beat up too much, so we took them into different realms where maybe they were a little scarier. We made them a little buffer and stronger-looking. More imposing. Some had more human heads, some had weird bird faces, some were in chains while others were not. They went through a lot of design iterations. Everything from dark crackling lava to an ash and charred-wood look. In the end, I think it ended up with something that was mostly dark, with a little bit of the ash helping to accentuate certain areas."

■ JOYNER

■ PREVIOUS JOYNER ▲ JOYNER

▲ JOYNER ▼ SUMMERS

▲ ▼ JOYNER

▲ SZE

▼ JOYNER

◄ SUMMERS

▲ JOYNER

▲ SUMMERS

"The cool thing about the fire demons, from an action point of view, is that when you hit these guys, you go straight through them," Morrison says. "So it's almost like you're taking a sort of fiery log, and then you're doing a karate punch through it. Not only does the log splinter into smithereens, but you also get a huge shower of sparks that travel away from the punch. So from an action-storytelling point of view, it's great because you can put Thor in the middle of a whole crowd of these attacking and just from where the showers of sparks are going—left, right, center, up, and down—you can actually tell which way he is punching or kicking. You also get to destroy them really well in a visually satisfying way."

◄ JOYNER ■ PREVIOUS JOYNER

▲ SUMMERS

JOYNER ▶

Surtur and his fire demons aren't the only creatures found on Muspelheim. Living deep below the planet's surface is a massive fire dragon—but not one audiences would expect. The filmmakers carefully crafted the beast, down to the inclusion of several unexpected elements. "The dragon looks great," Morrison says. "Basically, we've taken your traditional dragon, made the skin sort of like hardened lava, gave him eyes made of fire, and then gave him sort of retro-thruster jet packs. We went through a few rounds of design early on with wings made of fire, and it was all running into *Lord of the Rings* territory too quickly. So we wanted to come up with something much more interesting and decided to start with last principals first and go, 'Well, what does the dragon have to do? Thor can fly really fast, so we need a creature that can fly just that little bit faster than Thor, so when the Bifrost comes down, it saves him. Now, what's a really fast way to get around? Jetpacks, F-16 thrusters, fighter jets, that kind of stuff.' We kind of mounted big rocket thrusters on the back of a dragon, and then just for fun gave him sort of a fiery mohawk that runs all the way back down the center of his spine. It's pretty awesome, actually."

■ JOYNER

At one moment during the film's opening sequence, Thor points to the fire dragon and tells him to "stay." The VFX team took inspiration from that note for its take on the beast. "We've actually added an awful lot of dog performance into the dragon," Morrison says. "We've made it so when he picks up Thor in the beginning and shakes his head, it's like a dog picking up a squeaky toy. Except instead of a squeaky toy, it's a god."

■JOYNER

JOYNER

■ JOYNER

BEN-MIMOUN ▶

▲ HEFFERNAN

▲ HEFFERNAN

▲ **JOYNER**

"The fire dragon was one of my favorite things to work on," Joyner says. "We did so many versions of this thing where it went from a really weird wyvern to a kind of 'bad' luck dragon, up to the final design. The interesting thing was we backwards-engineered it a little bit. The image of the severed head, which we knew would be a big gag in the movie, was the first one I did of the final design. Once that was approved, I began working backwards on that and started asking questions: 'What does the body for that head look like?' In the end, we came up with this creature without any wings on it. It was powered by the flame within rather than a traditional winged dragon, but there are enough elements that it is pretty recognizable."

BEN-MIMOUN ▶

HELA

GODDESS OF DEATH

After defeating Surtur, Thor returns to Asgard for the first time since the end of *Thor: The Dark World*. Loki has been ruling in the guise of Odin, but has become careless in his portrayal. Sensing a change in his father, Thor quickly discovers that his brother has been masquerading as the king.

Learning his father is still alive and banished, powerless, on Earth, Thor travels to Midgard with Loki to search for him. But before they can return him to Asgard, they are confronted by a new and powerful enemy: Hela!

"One of the first things that happens when he sees Hela is that we discover she has the power to lift the hammer, even destroy the hammer," Executive Producer Brad Winderbaum says. "Now we're left with a powerless Thor. He can't summon lightning like he used to. He can't cause earthquakes like he used to."

Struggling with his own worthiness, Thor must discover who he really is. "What we have is the setup of this character journey," Winderbaum says, "where Thor is going to have to eventually face off with his doubts. 'Am I my father? Am I the man my father wants me to be? Or am I my own man? Am I my own king?' And that's the most important thing. That's the thing that's going to save the universe at the end."

LOKI

Up to his old mischief is Thor's adoptive brother, Loki. While he retains his traditional green-and-gold color palette, the *Thor: Ragnarok* filmmakers decided to have a bit more fun with his costume. "One question with Loki was if he should keep the same Loki look, or be more like one of the characters of Sakaar," Concept Artist Anthony Francisco says. "As the idea was that Loki was trying to get close to the Grandmaster, we ended up exploring a more Sakaaran design for his costume, using a lot of Jack Kirby's shapes and colors. Initially, we played with his iconic green, but soon we did more passes on crazy colors and combinations for his costume."

■ **FRANCISCO**

■ PREVIOUS **MARVEL STUDIOS PRODUCTION STILL** WITH **DEL RE**

▲ FRANCISCO

▲ BACALLADO

■ FRANCISCO

■ FRANCISCO

Francisco was excited to create a new helmet for Loki, exploring several concepts with more Nordic designs and spiraled-horn variations. Ultimately, he looked to his childhood for inspiration. "What's cool with the new Loki helmet design is that we made it with an open top with his hair showing, which has always been the way I had seen Loki when I was younger and going through the X-Men 'Asgardian Wars' comics," Francisco says. "It was a childhood image that has always been in my head that I wanted to implement, and luckily the design I did was chosen. Having that new helmet helps him look really different from the way he was before."

FRANCISCO ▶

■ FRANCISCO

While Loki's weapons of choice are trickery and manipulation, he isn't afraid to use something with a bit more bite when the occasion demands it. "Loki's daggers were a really fun one to work on," Concept Artist Jake Hempson says. "I did loads of iterations, initially working on more traditional Asgardian designs, but later switching to a more Sakaaran style. I moved away from the previous daggers seen in the other films to something inspired by modern military knife designs with a Kirby twist. An intentionally geometric and hard-edged blade suits Loki's personality. I suggested the idea of having Loki's throwing daggers as twin-pronged blades, which came to me as a kind of cruel idea that Loki might want to break off the thinner blade section in an adversary. Basically, a dual-edged piece of nastiness. Just like Loki."

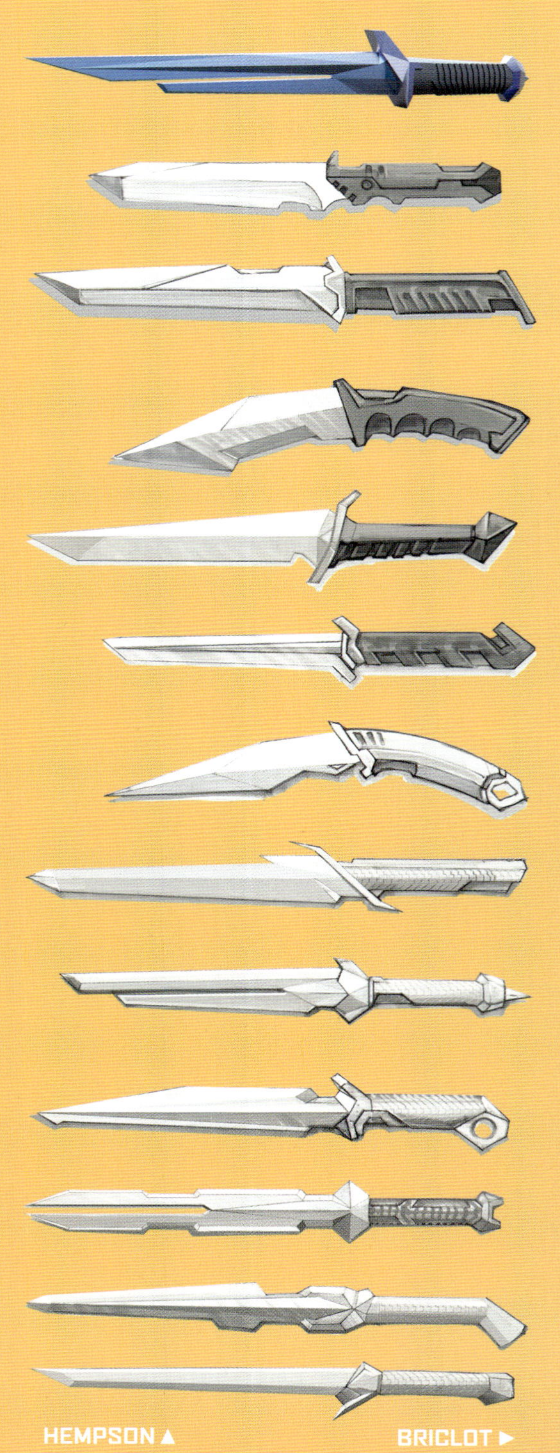

HEMPSON ▲

BRICLOT ►

◄ BRICLOT

▲ BACALLADO

Creating Odin's look was not as straightforward as in previous films, as the design had to take Loki's sensibilities into account. "The first time we see Odin, he is at a party. And it isn't really him. It is an impersonation by Loki," Costume Designer Mayes C. Rubeo says. "Loki had his own view of how he would dress in that moment. So it wasn't all gold like we always portray Odin. He was in a more festive mode, drinking wine and having all the crème de la crème of Asgard looking at this play that was made and invented by him."

◄ **SZE** ■ PREVIOUS **HEFFERNAN**

▲ HEFFERNAN

▲ ▶ BACALLADO

HELA

Designing Hela, the film's main antagonist, was no small task. Even in a fantasy-based world, concept and visual-effects artists had to find balance in a costume that could easily have crossed the line of believability. "Hela was definitely the main thing I worked on for this film," Visual Development Supervisor Andy Park says. "A group of artists and I all did different takes on Hela before there was any casting or storylines into what or who she was. All we knew was the stuff from the comics—but as you know, like most of our films, it's not always a one-to-one adaptation. We are always respectful to the source material, but we're definitely creating it for the Marvel Cinematic Universe."

"For Hela's blades, I saw these as extensions and manifestations of herself and her power," Concept Designer Jake Hempson says. "As bitter, twisted, organic obsidian, barbed death shapes, flowing as lava-like tribal tattoos into her opponents. Occasionally, she could form more traditional sword-like shapes for her amusement, as there would be no real need for her to fight conventionally, doing it solely for her own enjoyment."

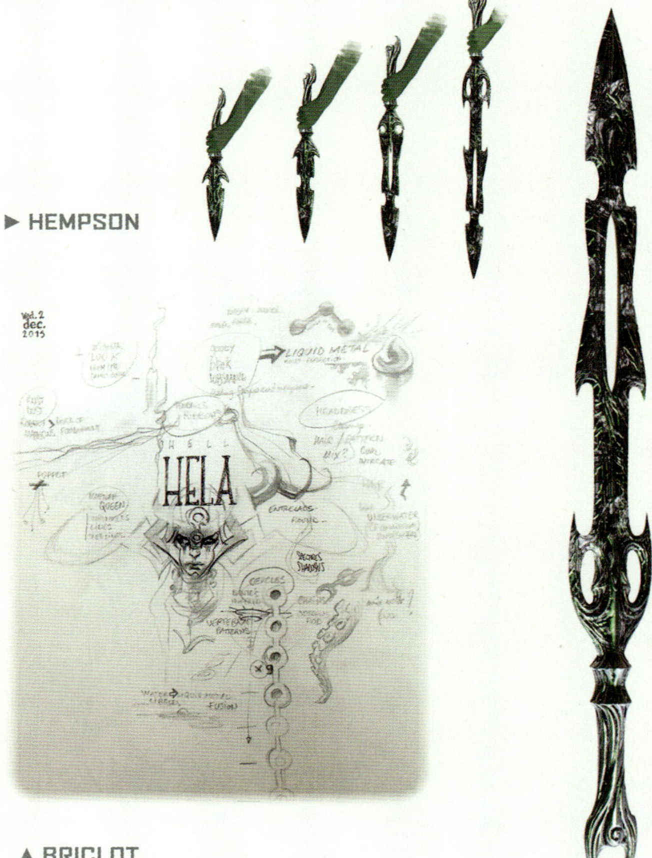

► HEMPSON

▲ BRICLOT

■ PARK

▲ PARK

▲ JOYNER

"The signature look for Hela in the comics is her headdress," Park says. "It looks great on those pages as a 2D element, but whenever we design something for our films, we're thinking thinking believability. It's going to be on a real actress, so how do we do that? You definitely want to see the full design on screen, but you don't want to laugh at it, either. Because of that, a lot of the early versions I did had more believable, smaller antlers. Of course, it was pretty clear that the filmmakers were gravitating toward the bigger, truer-to-comics-style headdresses, so it became a task of finding the right ratio of antler to body. She was definitely a huge design challenge, but probably one of the more exciting challenges in all my seven-plus years being here at Marvel Studios."

▲ PARK

JOYNER ▲

PARK

■ PARK

■ PARK

"Origin stories are so useful because there's this long, deep history between a lot of these characters," Cate Blanchett says. "And particularly for a character like me who comes out of nowhere. It's not like she's appeared quietly in a couple of other films. Some people have a knowledge of her. Some people won't actually know her at all. You have to strike a balance between those fans who do know her and those who don't. So you can be mysterious, but also give enough backstory that you understand why the character does what she does. Because I think the best villains are always those that you kind of love and hate what they do, but you sort of understand it. There's a logic to it. They're not just completely nuts."

■ BACALLADO

■ PARK

■ PARK

■ BRICLOT

"Her costume is going to tie directly into her power itself," Executive Producer Brad Winderbaum says. "If you remember Gorr the God Butcher, from the Jason Aaron run of *Thor: God of Thunder*—he picked up a godly weapon and it infected him, almost like the Venom symbiote from the Spider-Man books, allowing his character to change and create new weapons and create new wardrobes for himself throughout. And that's what Hela's going to do."

■ **BRICLOT**

■ FRANCISCO

▲ PARK

▲ MEINERDING

"Hela feels abandoned by Odin," Winderbaum says. "She comes from a time that predates Thor, Loki, and Heimdall. A time of old Asgard when Odin was more of an Old Testament, fire-and-brimstone type of ruler who took over the Nine Realms as a conqueror, and Hela was his right hand—his executioner.

"She was born with a rare gift to create infinite, terrible, deadly weapons at her whim, and he turned her into a powerful weapon of war. And together they carried out a conquest of the Nine Realms. Time passes. Odin grows older and has more clarity. He realizes the ruler he wants to be. The world he wants to foster. He becomes a more benevolent king. He earns the moniker of the All-Father as a life-bringing force to the universe. And this weapon of war that Hela was no longer has a place in this new world."

■ ORTIZ

FRANCISCO

Not all elements conceptualized during the filmmaking process are used in the final product. While Hela is powerful enough to conquer Asgard on her own, the first group of minions designed to aid the Goddess of Death in her quest were the Butchers, creatures formed and animated by her powers to do her bidding. "We did a lot of explorations on these characters," Concept Artist Ian Joyner says. "I had three designs that seemed to resonate. One was more humanoid, one was a little bit more creature-like, and another was a full-on creature with tails and the whole works.

"To help with contrast, we then did explorations in white. I tried to keep some of the dark greens in the extremities, and then have the brightness happen in the faces and the bodies and let them pop out. I referenced all sorts of different things when designing them, from butterflies to orcas, just playing in paint and seeing which ones looked fun."

■ JOYNER

◄ SUMMERS

▲ JOYNER

▲ JOYNER

▲ JOYNER

▲ BRICLOT

◄ BRICLOT

▲ FRANCISCO

"Originally, we had Butchers in the film, and the Butchers were born of Hela's power," Visual Effects Supervisor Jake Morrison says. "The idea was that she would gesture and there would be a connection between her and the ground, and then these creatures would grow from that connection. But during the course of developing the film, we discovered that it was actually more interesting to do something else entirely."

▲ HEMPSON

SUMMERS ►

■ JOYNER

■ JOYNER

Replacing the defunct Butcher concept would be the Dead Guards, or D-Guards. "These are the people that helped Hela conquer the Nine Realms thousands of years ago, and they're just decomposed corpses at the bottom of a pit," Morrison says. "So she dives down, reincarnates them all, and they all come back to life. It's effectively a zombie army based around E-Guards, the Einherjar."

"You can see some of the earlier head studies where I was blending in the Butchers," Joyner says. "The idea was to take the E-Guard design and manipulate that, and explore everything from them being very human and having their skeletons fused into that armor, all the way up to them turning into some form of the Butcher. Some were faceless jack-o'-lantern-style beings, while others were more zombified, all powered by this ethereal energy."

■ SUMMERS

■ CORDELLA

■ PREVIOUS **SZE**

SKURGE

"We're really excited to bring Skurge to the Cinematic Universe," Brad Winderbaum says. "He is one of the most iconic characters in the Thor pantheon and has one of the most iconic moments in comic-book history. In the books, Skurge is a villain typically. He was a villain through most of his time as a Marvel character, and in the end, he dies doing something incredibly heroic to save Thor and save the universe."

When designing the Executioner, Mayes C. Rubio didn't have to look far for inspiration. "With Skurge, we wanted to be faithful to his iconic character from the comics," Rubeo says. "It was blue, broad shoulders, almost like a Roman costume—interesting, vain, self-indulgent. We worked on that costume a lot because we wanted to find the right color and the right dimensions for him without exaggerating."

▲ HEMPSON

▼ FRANCISCO

▲ BACALLADO

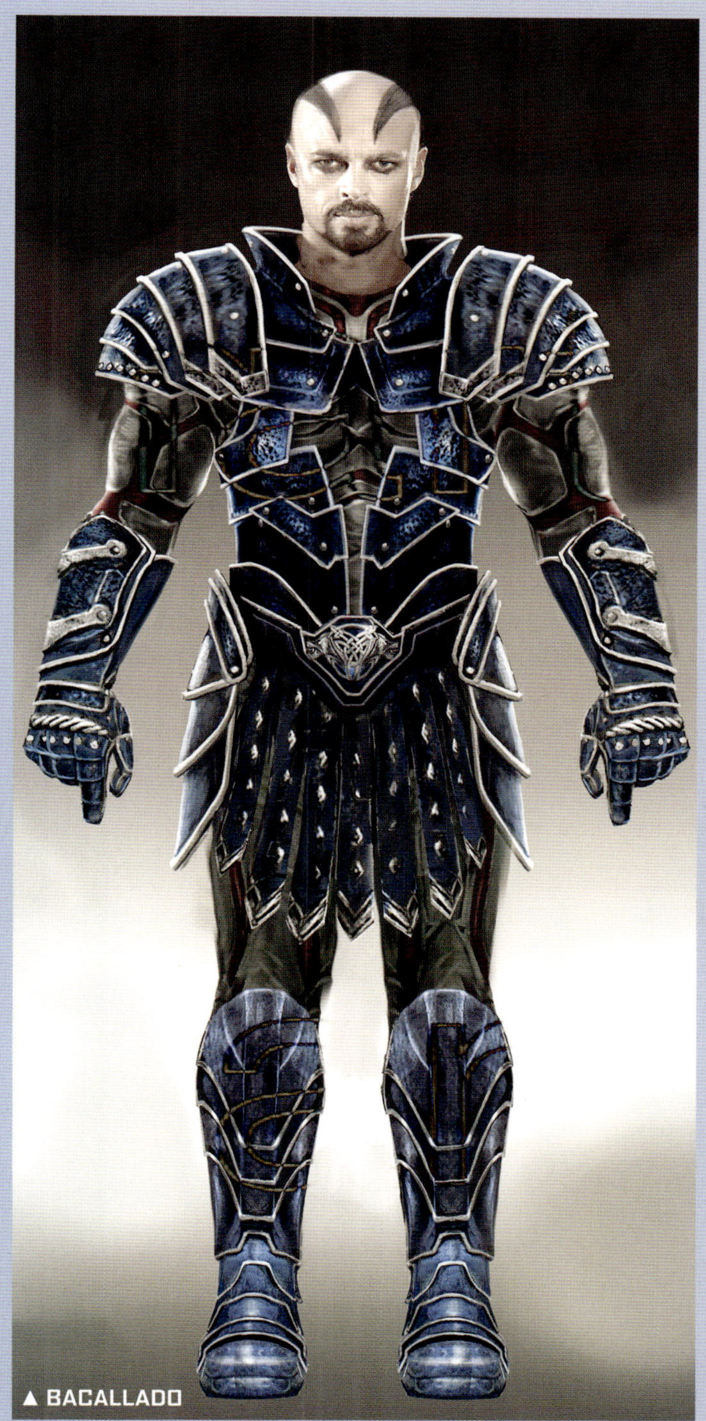

▲ BACALLADO

EINHERJAR

The Einherjar have been seen in both *Thor* and *Thor: The Dark World*, but their purpose was somewhat utilitarian. In this film, Asgard's army of elite warriors takes center stage in a pivotal first-act sequence. "When Hela first returns to Asgard, she is confronted by the entire Einherjar army," Brad Winderbaum says. "This is her first major test of strength, and we get to see just how deadly she can be. During the battle, she conjures an endless supply of incredible weapons and decimates the entire E-Guard legion, solidifying her position and demonstrating the massive amounts of power she possesses. When audiences watch this sequence, it's easy to see why she used to strike fear in the hearts of people all over the Nine Realms."

DIAZ

■ BACALLADO

The epic showdown between Hela and the Einherjar ends quickly—with an exclamation point. Easily decimated by the goddess, hundreds of soldiers lay in piles on the streets of Asgard. "I was asked to create a frame in which Hela would resemble a 'pincushion of spears' after fighting the Einherjar, wading through a sea of Einherjar bodies," Concept Artist Michael Kutsche says. "So I did two sketches, one of them a top view with only the pile of fallen Einherjar filling out the whole frame and Hela standing in midst of it, and the other one became the basis for the final version. Since she is not feeling any pain from the spears, and because she is not emotionally affected by the situation at all, I put her in a pose that is almost catwalk-like, which underlines her superiority. In the background is the golden tower of Asgard, which reflects the sunset and is partially dipped in red shadows, meant to set the right atmosphere and to enhance her dark silhouette."

◄ **ALLAN**

HEFFERNAN ▲

▲ REES

▲ HEMPSON

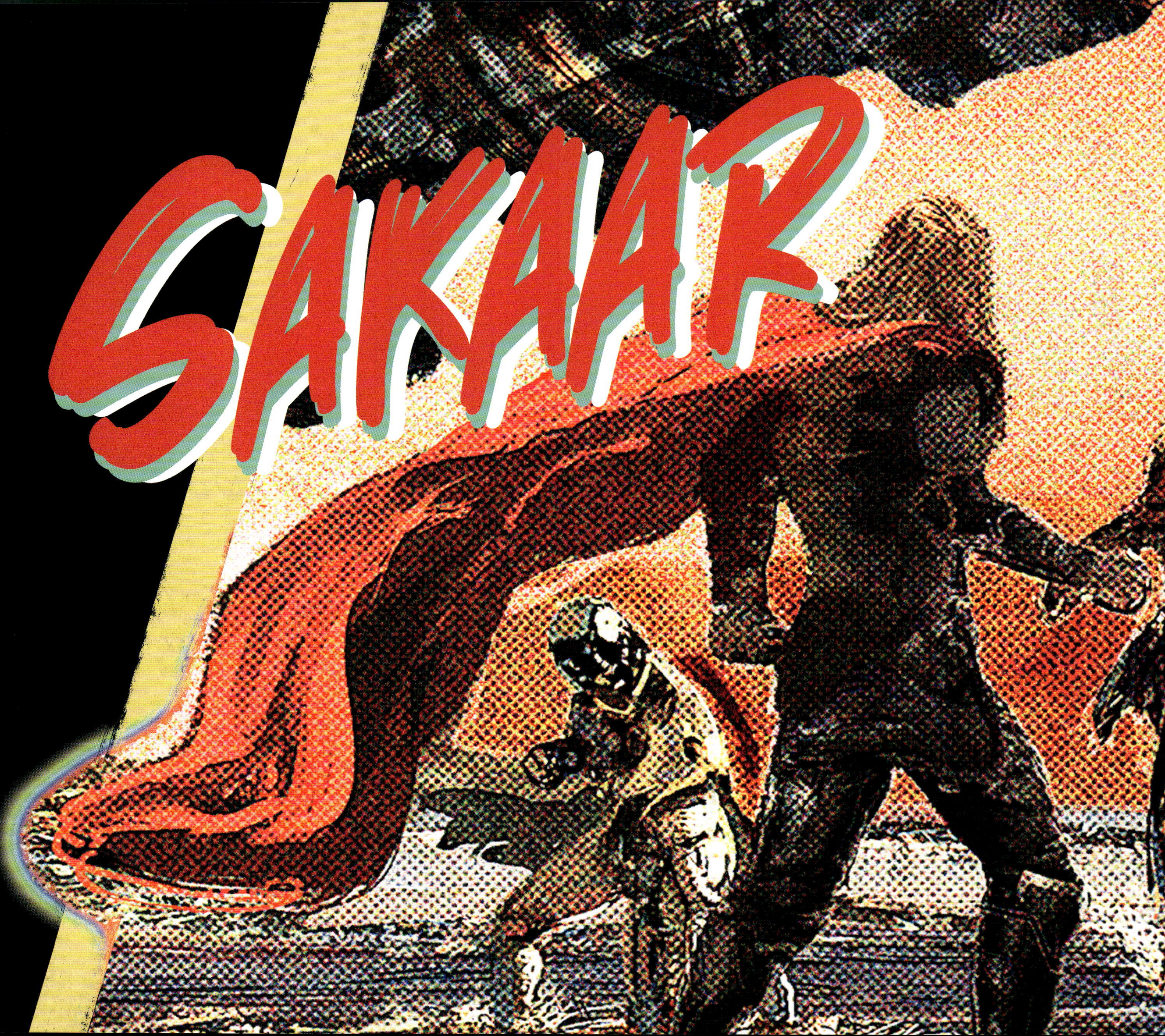
SAKAAR

Having been ejected from the Bifrost during his confrontation with Hela, Thor emerges from a wormhole on the far side of the universe, deposited on a strange new planet. Immediately, his focus becomes singular: He must return to Asgard and defeat this new enemy. All he has to do first is figure out where he is.

"Sakaar is potentially in another galaxy," Production Designer Dan Hennah says. "It's a planet that is in the center of a whole bunch of wormholes. These wormholes gather space debris from out in the universe, and it all ends up landing on the surface of Sakaar and has been for thousands of years. So basically the surface, while it was maybe rock or dirt or whatever, has got a layer of debris, especially where the wormholes are, that may be hundreds of meters thick in some places."

Finding the way back to Asgard won't be easy. Almost immediately after crash-landing on the planet's surface, Thor is confronted by a band of scrappers. "They are these creatures that live on the outskirts of the main city of Sakaar and collect all the valuable things that fall out of these giant wormholes in the sky," Executive Producer Brad Winderbaum says. "And sometimes, those valuable things are people."

Thor is no stranger to the various realms, but he's never seen a world quite like Sakaar. As he slowly discovers the strange planet, so too will the audience. "The wonderful thing about *Thor: Ragnarok* is that we get to experience a whole world that we've never seen before," Production Designer Ra Vincent says. "We plunge ourselves deep into the very root of the inspiration, which was Jack Kirby's illustrations that were generated over 30 and 40 years ago.

"We're imparting his designs in not only an aesthetic sense, but also in a kind of whole-world ethos. We're bringing that into a real-world environment now and landing in an alien planet, which in this case is Sakaar, with all of Jack Kirby's influence building toward that final look. We're exploring a completely new realm that I don't think cinema has ever seen before."

■ 118-119 **SZE**, 120-121 **KUTSCHE**, 122-123 **BEN-MIMOUN** WITH **DEL RE**

▲ **BEN-MIMOUN**
HEFFERNAN ▶

■ BACALLADO

■ BACALLADO

▲ BRICLOT

▲ BACALLADO

▲ BACALLADO

▲ FRANCISCO

▲ BRICLOT

GARY ▲

▲ RIHAL

Being a scrapper is no easy life. After scavenging the wasteland for valuable items fallen from the wormholes, they need to transport their newly found treasures back to the city for market. To fulfill that requirement, the scrapper vessel is modular, composed of smaller ships that can detach and reattach for ease of access.

"Ultimately, the scrapper vehicle is our way of honoring the majesty of the random shapes in Jack Kirby art by recreating some of those two-dimensional pictures into three-dimensional objects," Vincent says. "You'll notice that if you try and emulate Jack Kirby's drawing style, you find yourself just responding very intuitively to changes in direction. The more responsive you can be to an intuitive approach, the more Jack Kirby-esque your objects become. And it was Taika's instructions about polystyrene inserts in cardboard boxes that really gave us the direction that we needed to go in in order to find Jack Kirby's approach to his illustrations.

"It's a kind of untold thinking that breeds amazing new ideas, and I think the scrappers' vehicle is pretty much the embodiment of the concept that you can develop something wonderful and new by reacting to a subconscious and sort of subliminal approach to design. Jack Kirby was so incredibly difficult to emulate that it wasn't until we experienced the freedom in choosing untold objects as the beginning for the vehicles that we really cracked it."

■ RIHAL

SCRAPPER 142

Going by the moniker of Scrapper 142, Valkyrie is as fierce a warrior as they come. Since escaping tragedy, Val has been shielding her identity while hiding out on Sakaar, slowly trying to drink her past into a distant memory. "Valkyrie is the last of the Valkyries—that is an elite regiment of Asgard," Costume Designer Mayes C. Rubeo says. "When she landed on Sakaar, she had to cope with the new world.

"While on Sakaar, she had to look very different. Now, she looks more or less Sakaaran. She's more like a scrapper herself. She has a very dark armor that is very utilitarian, very practical. She doesn't want to show off too much. She wants to be the person in the shadows that you don't see."

◄ SEKERIS

▲ BACALLADO

◀ MEINERDING

▲ SEKERIS

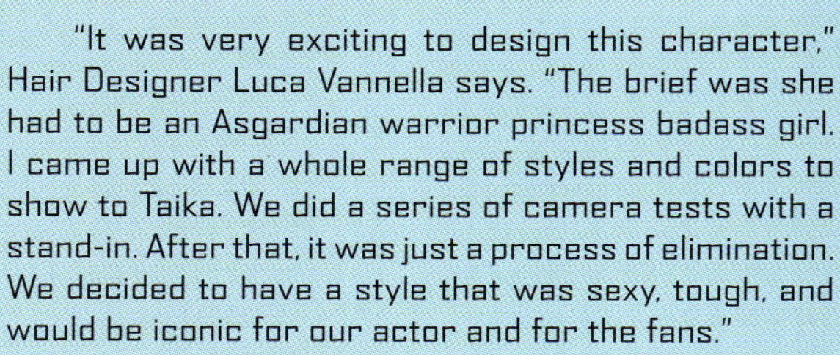

"It was very exciting to design this character," Hair Designer Luca Vannella says. "The brief was she had to be an Asgardian warrior princess badass girl. I came up with a whole range of styles and colors to show to Taika. We did a series of camera tests with a stand-in. After that, it was just a process of elimination. We decided to have a style that was sexy, tough, and would be iconic for our actor and for the fans."

◄▲ SEKERIS

▲ PARK

◄ ORTIZ

▲ SERKIS

▲ **PARK**

"Directors always get particularly excited about characters that they get to be the first to put on screen; you could tell Taika was very eager to tackle Valkyrie," Visual Development Supervisor Andy Park says. "He had a lot of ideas for her. He liked the idea that when she is first introduced, she is wearing some sort of tribal mask and hood, and that you don't necessarily know it's a woman. We did a lot of passes of her in her tribal-mask look, but ultimately the idea was not used in the film."

◄ **FRANCISCO**

With every hue of the spectrum a possibility for sets, vehicles, and costumes, teams needed to consider all color placement carefully to ensure balance. "When you get to coloring Sakaar, you have to make sure that it is a very restrained palette that you use," Visual Effects Supervisor Jake Morrison says. "For example, we're saying different districts of the city share a common hue. So if you were to stand back and look at the city from a super-wide angle, you would see common themes of color running through the different areas; if you vary it for one color per building, it would turn into this tutti-frutti absolute visual noise in a second."

■ PREVIOUS **BEN-MIMOUN**

BEN-MIMOUN ▲▼

BEN-MIMOUN ▲▼

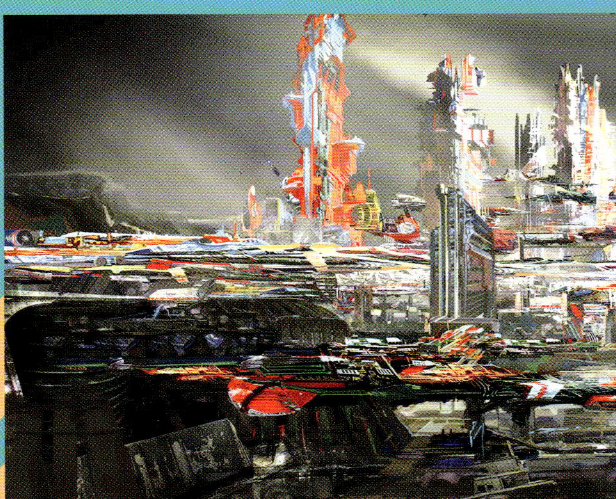

▼ SHUI

■ BEN-MIMOUN

▲ SUMMERS

▲ SCHIRLE

"We were able to help with the design of the palace, so I thought it would be cool to have the heroes of the arena immortalized Mount Rushmore-style on the building," Concept Artist Jackson Sze says. "The Hulk would be in progress, so audiences might catch that it's the Hulk, but Thor when he's flying in here might not necessarily or immediately know that it would be him."

▲ FRANCISCO  SZE ►

"Kirby had a little bit of a psychedelic feeling to his art, with more defined lines—not as vibrant, but just very colorful," Rubeo says. "When you put the world of Sakaar next to Asgard, they are completely opposite. Sakaar is not even a realm—it's just somewhere else. It's like outer space. It really felt like outer space for him when he landed there. It was like, 'Where am I? This is too crazy. There's too many colors. People have all these strange coifs.' And it was shocking for him."

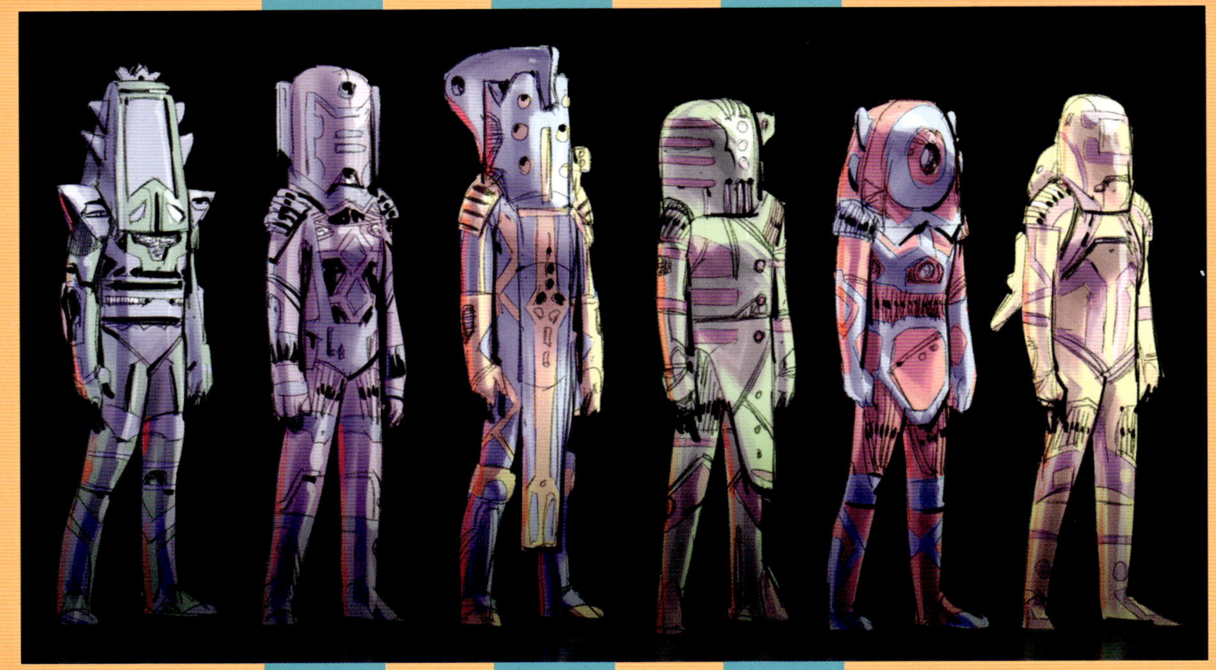

BACALLADO ▼

▲ HARRIS

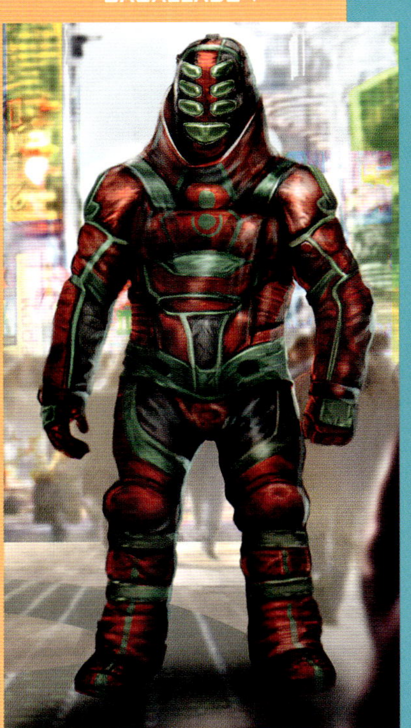

■ BACALLADO

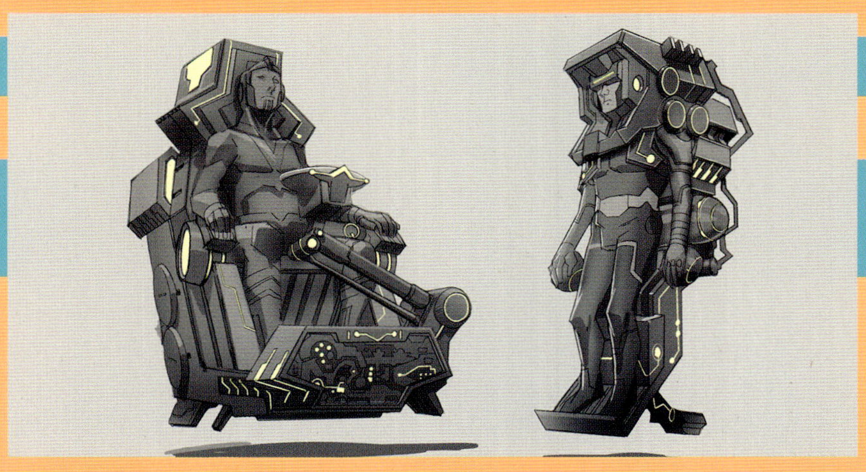
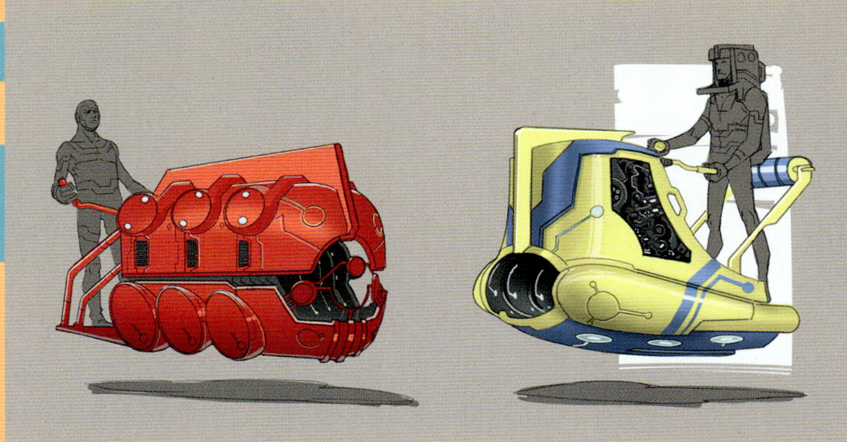

"Taking our original concept art, or taking Jack Kirby's influence, and then trying to manifest it as a real-life object is quite a journey," Production Designer Ra Vincent says. "It's taken our designers a long time to really kind of grapple with what exactly the language is. You can extrapolate from drawings and character, costumes, basic shapes, and things. But then it's the way that they are subtly portrayed in their color ways and some of the naïve lines that takes you back to the graphic content that is our base inspiration."

■ RUIZ

■ SEKERIS

THE

GRANDMASTER

Ruling over Sakaar is the Grandmaster, an overindulgent tyrant who prizes extravagance and luxury, and presides over Sakaar's Contest of Champions. "The Grandmaster was not an easy character to design," says Concept Artist Constantine Sekeris. "We explored many options, but ultimately, Andy Park, Kevin Feige, and Taika Waititi wanted to see a more grounded, realistic version. They wanted him to feel like he's obviously someone of status. They wanted some sort of cape. They wanted the textures and color palette retained from his original design from the comics—but again, update it for the Sakaar setting, and also kind of tie him to the character from the *Guardians of the Galaxy*, the Collector."

ORTIZ

SEKERIS ▲

ORTIZ ▶

▲ SZE

▲ BACALLADO

First appearing in *Avengers #69* in 1969, the Grandmaster has a rich history in the comics. "The Grandmaster is a tyrannical leader on a planet where people don't have a lot of personal freedom," Executive Producer Brad Winderbaum says. "But he is also the ringleader of the circus. And in a planet where anything can fall out of the sky and crush you from one of these wormholes at any time, he is there to kind of distract you from your imminent mortality with these giant games and events.

Bringing the Grandmaster to life on the big screen is actor Jeff Goldblum. "We wanted that character to be really memorable and really fun," Winderbaum says. "And Taika had the vision for Goldblum, and it was just perfect. He's musical, he's whimsical, he's got a strong presence while still being hilarious, and he can play in this alien world really well. He's got one of the most memorable voices in the film."

◄ SEKERIS

▲KUTSCHE

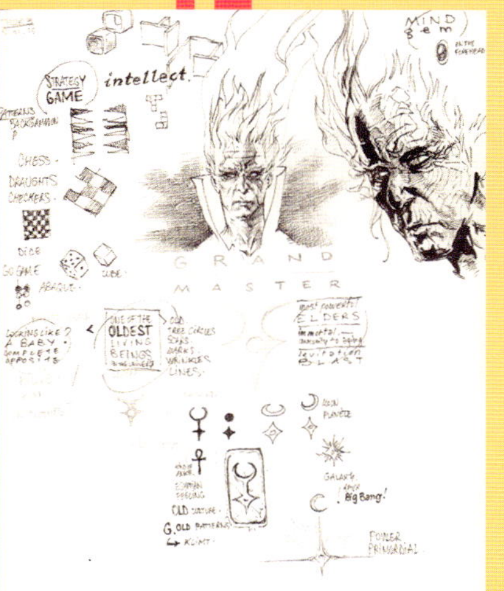

"A recurring challenge for the visual development of the MCU is to design new, believable, and attractive looks for colorful and often over-the-top comic-book characters," Concept Artist Aleksi Briclot says. "How do you create a new appearance with this exuberant blue-and-yellow Grandmaster that will be suitable in a movie? I started with my sketchbook, creating a mindmap—basically taking notes of character key words, adding references, and jotting down other ideas that could pop in my mind during the exercise.

"As one of the oldest living beings in the universe, and given his penchant to build complex strategy, I thought about Dracula. And then the yellow color becoming gold seemed a good way to add some preciosity and pompousness to the look. Then Gustav Klimt entered into the process, and then some haute-couture references to help define the cool and majestic patterns."

HEFFERNAN

▲HARGREAVES

▲HEFFERNAN

◄ SZE

▲ BACALLADO

▲MACKIE

The Grandmaster's right hand, Topaz, was an unexpected addition to *Thor: Ragnarok*. "Topaz is one of those characters that evolved during the design phase," says Concept Artist Jonay Bacallado. "In the beginning, she didn't even have lines in the script or a name. But during the development process, Topaz became much more interesting and added weight to the story. She was smart and funny. She would pilot ships and speak her mind. So taking those elements into consideration, we translated that into the shape, form, and silhouette you get to see in the film.

"Her overall design was based on the Grandmaster's guards, one of the first things we came up with for Sakaar. The guards defined many design elements for this world, with most of its inspiration coming from Kirby and his Celestials. For Topaz, color was vital for the audience to immediately recognize her when she is among the crowd. There are no other guards in the film using her color combination in order to give her a uniqueness and sense of higher rank."

▲BACALLADO

▲BACALLADO

BACALLADO

"The Grandmaster's guards are probably the characters with the most design revisions done for the film," Bacallado says. "Taika had a very specific vision, based on Kirby's artwork. In the final designs for the guards at the Grandmaster's palace, colors were kept to two-tone combinations of primary and secondary colors, plus blacks and grays so they would read well against the scenery. The helmets were designed to remove any humanness from their faces—so the composition of the shapes, plus a smart use of lighter and darker values, created depth and interest in their design. The change of the design also affected the construction process, going from softer materials to more sculpted, technical pieces. The Grandmaster's guards ended up with very complex specialty costumes, with every detail finely sculpted, cast, and painted in the same level of finish as the main characters."

■ BACALLADO

■ BACALLADO

"The designs were at first less anatomical—big helmets, no human expressions, disproportioned arms, bold and bright colors, and geometrical patterns creating striking color combinations," Bacallado says. "Sometimes, they incorporated bold geometric shapes into the designs—so instead of, for example, having a glove or a gauntlet, the character had spheres for hands. As we continued designing, we realized some of those shapes would be difficult for actors and stuntmen to perform in, so we kept the Kirby-esque motifs in order to accommodate this need. But from the many designs options we had, we chose the ones that could be more practical in terms of movement."

▼▲ CORDELLA

▼ DIAZ

■ CORDELLA

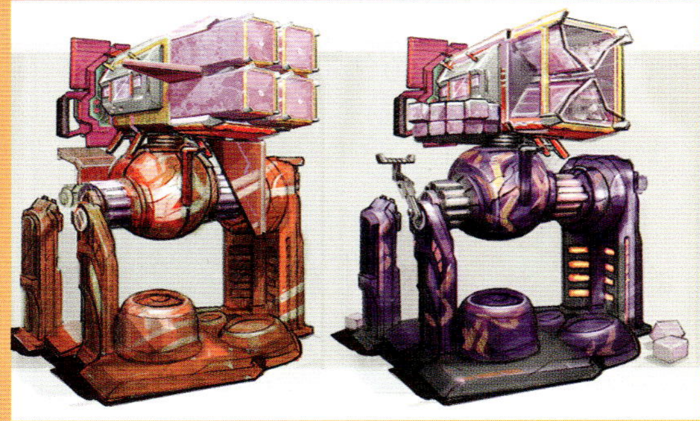

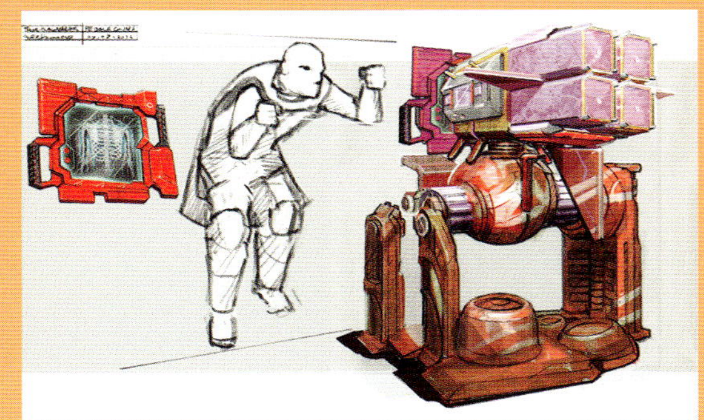

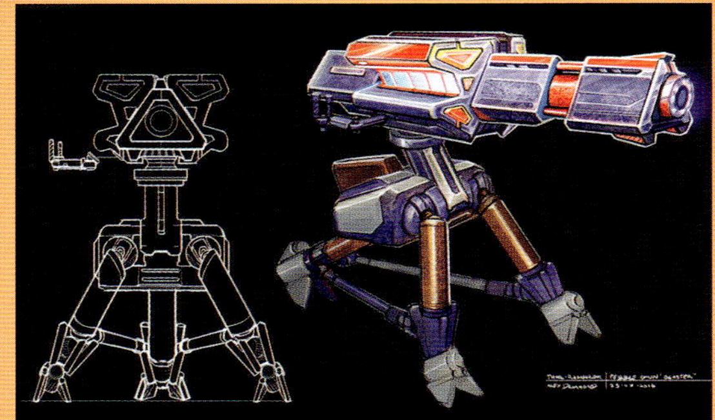

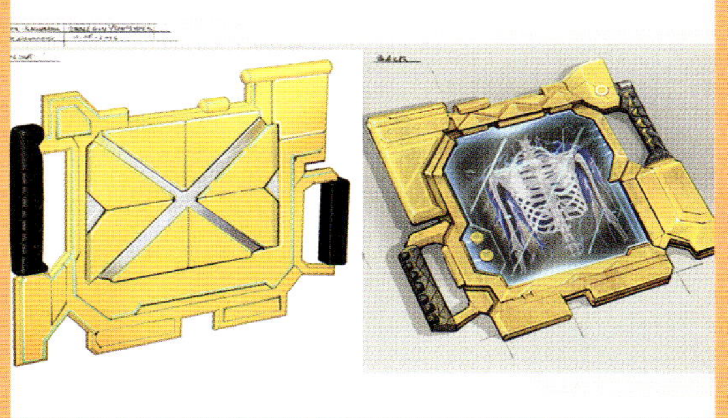

"These are the designs for the Pebble Gun used by the Grandmaster," Props Illustrator Alex Drummond says. "As with most of my prop work, I immediately hit the traditional sketchbook using my fast marker technique, which involves iterative sketching while talking with the production lead. I would sketch around 30 to 40 thumbnails before Production Designer Dan Hennah would drop by to check if I was on track. Then I scanned everything and began to refine in Photoshop using my custom marker brush set. I like to explore as many variations on an idea in fast-sketch mode as I can. This project was a prop illustrator's dream job."

"In a funny sort of way, time was on our side for the design of the glassware, because we had exhausted so much time on set design and dressing and furniture design that the most domestic and mundane objects had very little time for full consideration," Production Designer Ra Vincent says. "So part of the design was purely functional. We had a collection of motifs by the time we got to creating the glassware, so if we could think of a way of assembling these motifs into usable objects, maybe that was a nice, quick way around it. And purely by accident, the moment you assemble all these cool Kirby-inspired shapes and motifs into, say, a plate or a martini glass, you've just ended up with something that's pretty off the wall and super-reminiscent of all the kind of architectural details and all the furniture design. All of a sudden, you get a crazy-cool common language for every object in Sakaar."

■ DRUMMOND

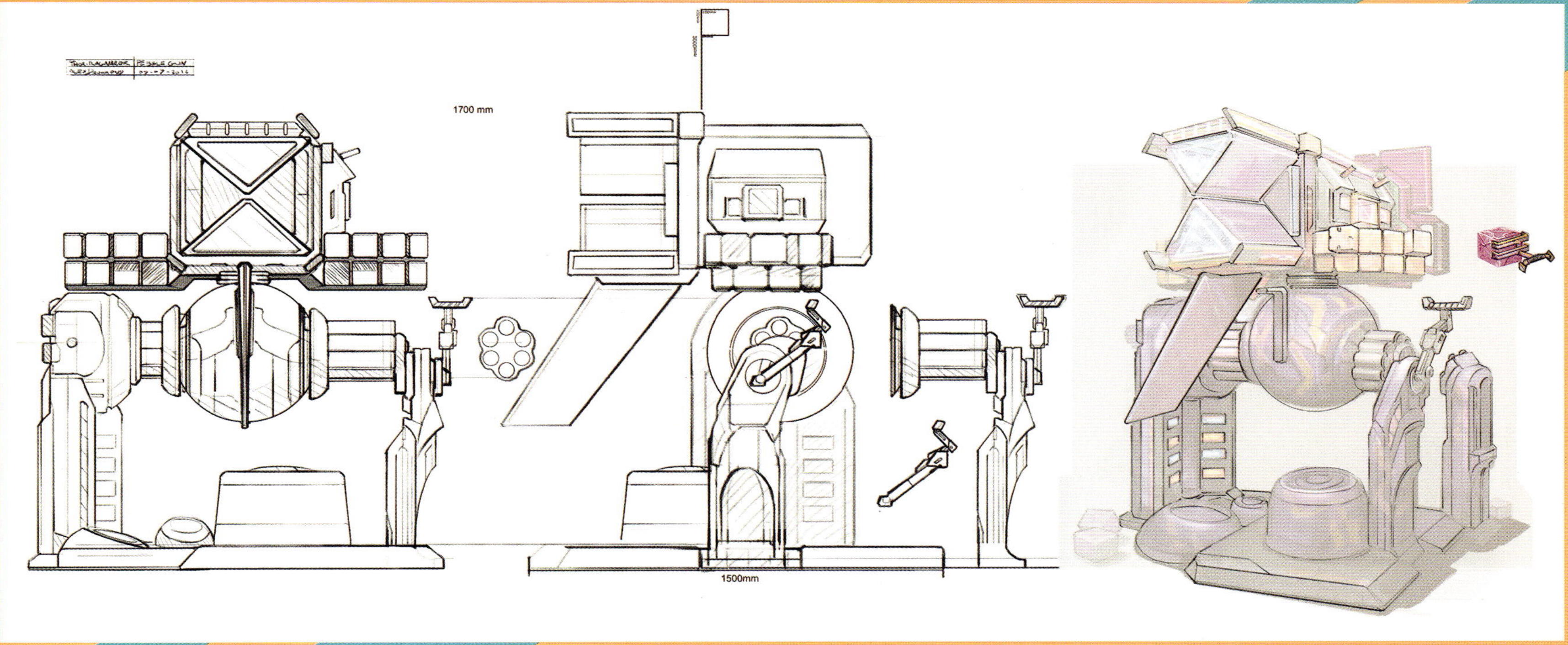

1700 mm

1500mm

■ DRUMMOND

Contest of Champions

We have a new contender! After being captured and sold to the Grandmaster for an exorbitant sum, Thor finds himself forced to fight as a gladiator in the Contest of Champions. Sakaaran citizens fill the stadium as he prepares for battle. His hair is shorn and his clothing made battle-ready for the arena's blue sands.

"The Grandmaster is a fantastic character from the Marvel Universe," Director Taika Waititi says. "He's quite an eccentric character. He loves pitting heroes against each other, and one of the big things that he would do in the comics was a thing called the Contest of Champions, where you would take favorite heroes and make them play games or make them fight. And we're doing our own spin on that where he is the master of Sakaar, the world that Thor finds himself on, and Thor must fight through this Contest of Champions to get out of Sakaar and win his freedom. So Thor must win his freedom by fighting his old friend: the Incredible Hulk!"

They may be pals, but Thor wouldn't like Hulk when he's angry. "The Hulk that Thor meets in the arena is a Hulk that's been the Hulk for a longer period of time than ever before," Executive Producer Brad Winderbaum says. "He hasn't been Bruce Banner since Natasha threw him over that cliff at the end of *Avengers: Age of Ultron*. Now, he's been Hulk so long that he can talk a little bit. He can create these rudimentary sentences. He can communicate with Thor. But Thor makes the big mistake of calling him Banner, and nothing makes Hulk angrier than the name Bruce Banner."

"When you look at the design of this whole place, it is entirely a tribute to the artistry of Jack Kirby," President of Marvel Studios and Executive Producer Kevin Feige says. "The entire design, from the costumes to these walls to the little props, is entirely an unabashed tribute to Jack Kirby. Obviously, none of us here at Marvel Studios would be doing what we do without Jack Kirby.

"And all of the *Thor* films have always been inspired by his work, the Avengers films, the *Iron Man* films—but in this particular movie, Taika had an idea to just really make it a tribute and take it as close as we could get to his design style from the comics and not just use them for tonal inspiration. And the lines that you see are in many cases taken directly from his panels. It's almost a surreal experience walking around, as if we had finally, after so many years, stepped into a Jack Kirby drawing."

■ PREVIOUS **GRAY** WITH **DEL RE**

■ **SHIU**

▲ HEFFERNAN

▲ KATTIE

Deep below the arena are the catacombs, where gladiators await their chance for glory—or death. "The holding area set was this place where the bounty hunters bring in people they have discovered who have just recently landed, and they get sold in there into a form of slavery until they're processed," Production Designer Dan Hennah says. "They can become gladiators if they have any potential. And of course Thor had potential.

"They get accepted in this particular area or get put into a holding cell, which is our big curved holding cell. And then they get taken out of the holding cell and processed—haircut, all that stuff, given the armor, given the swords, whatever they want to fight with. And then they go off from that cell into the arena on their fight day to do their best."

■ RUIZ

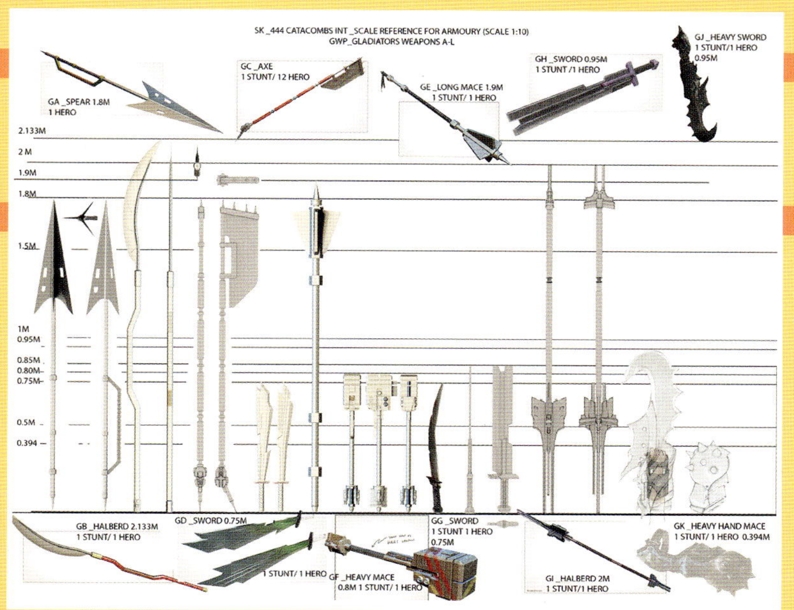

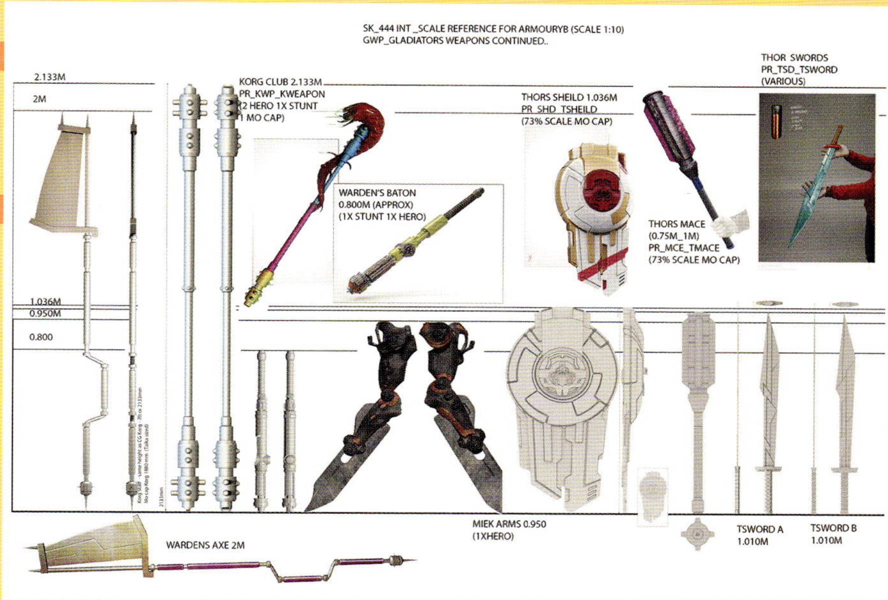

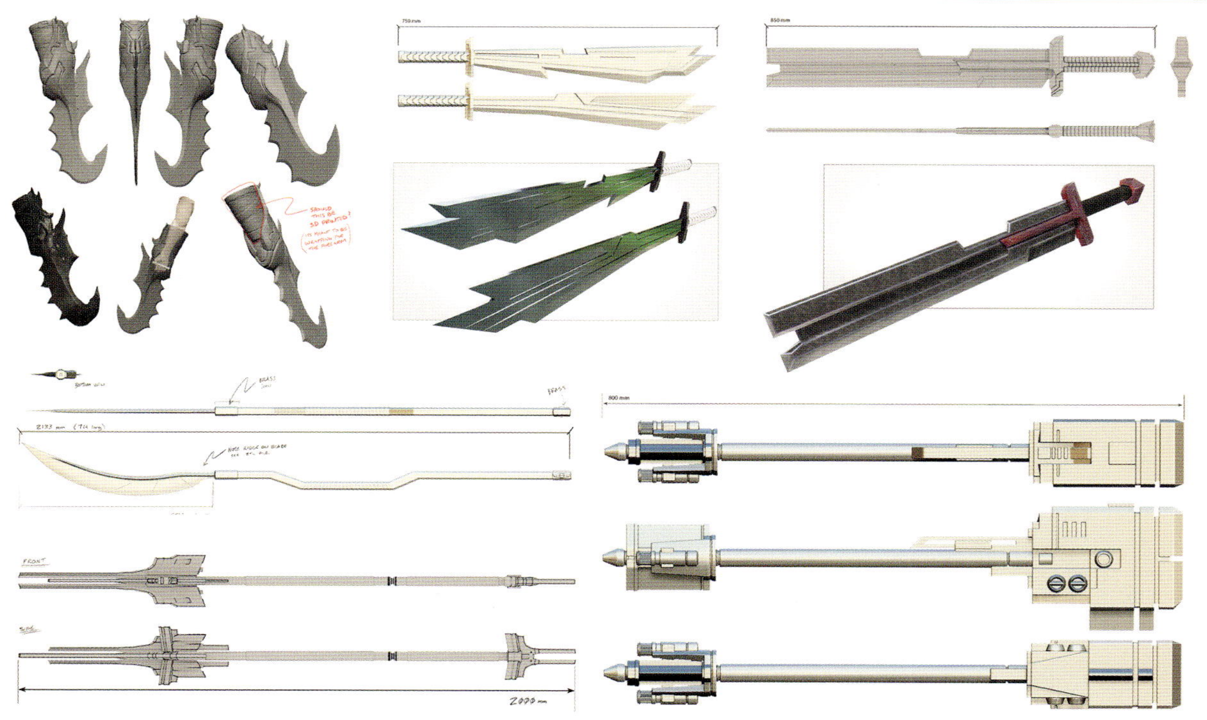

■ HEMPSON

"The gladiator weapons were designed to match the palette of their costumes, all having a base geometric Sakaaran feel to them," Concept Artist Jake Hempson says. "Others were more scrapper-like, as if they were a hand-painted engine part, or a drive from a spaceship re-used as a hammer. Everything from the Sakaar world had to have a Jack Kirby feel to it."

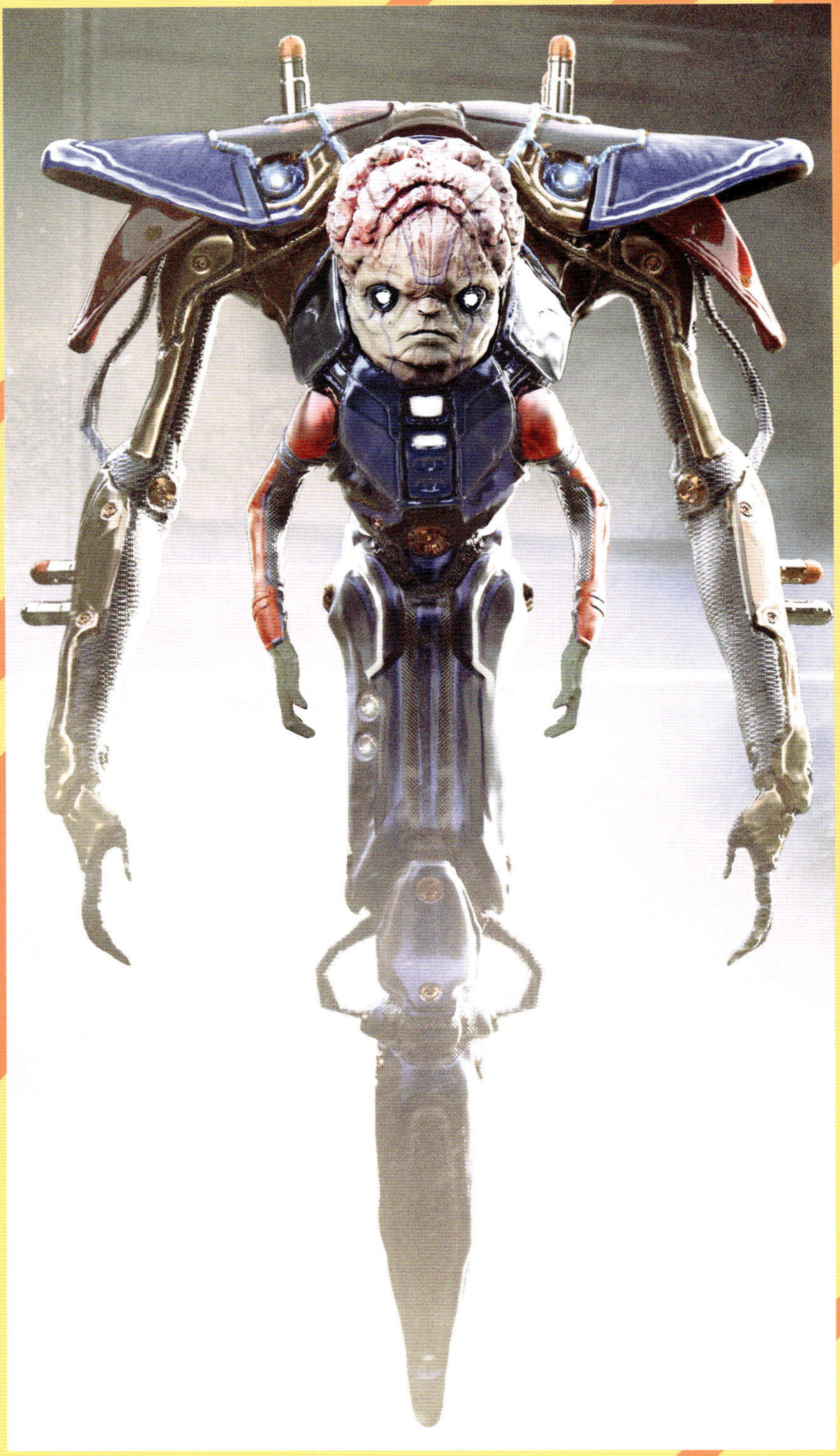

■ SEKERIS

■ KUTSCHE

KORG

"How do you go about bringing the fully digital speaking rock man that just to happens to be played by our director, Taika Waititi, to life? Very carefully," Visual Effects Supervisor Jake Morrison says. "It's interesting. He's a great character. He's a favorite for all the VFX crews, and I'm sure he will be for audiences, too.

"From a visual point of view, he's an incredible challenge. In animation, there is classic squash-and-stretch animation where as a creature moves, they slightly change profile or their skin stretches. If you're made of rocks, you can't do that because the first thing that happens is that it looks like latex. Because if a rock gets bigger, you know that it can't be made of rock. So what has to happen is we have to go through and consider every possible expression that may be performed, and then backtrack from there and make sure that when we build him, we cut him into fine enough pieces to make sure that he can deliver all those lines and expressions. From a technical point of view, it's extraordinarily complicated."

▲ SUMMERS

▲▶ JOYNER

◀ SUMMERS ▲ HEMPSON

▲ SUMMERS

"I've done quite a few rock monsters over the years," Concept Artist Tully Summers says. "Whether it's a practical suit, or a completely digital creation, the problem is always that squishy stretching rocks in motion ruin the illusion, and it's not rock anymore. The challenge then is to come up with enough rock seams and separations to allow for proper movement, while still showing a convincing form that conveys character. I took extra care with the seams on Korg's face, and tried to indicate enough pieces so the VFX folks could shift them believably into various expressions.

"I was thrilled when I found out Taika chose to play him! I originally gave Korg some classic gladiator armor, all straps and plates. Then Taika requested a design pass where he's wearing Stubbies, a type of short shorts guys wear in New Zealand. The result was a sci-fi Stubbies/wife-beater onesie with Taika's sly humor."

MIEK

Often found in Korg's company is his best buddy, Miek. "The cool thing about Miek is he's two completely different creatures in one," Morrison says. "If you look at him from a distance, he's a robot killing machine. He's basically an exoskeleton with three-foot-long blades for arms. But if you start looking closely, you can see that in the center of the exoskeleton, there's a purple slug. And if you look even closer than that, you'll actually see that he's got these tiny little appendages that run up and down his body. And if you look even closer still, you'll see that the little appendages at the top have little fingers moving tiny joysticks to drive the exoskeleton. It's almost like the giant mech that Ripley gets into at the end of *Aliens*, but it's a slug doing the driving. He's pretty fun, I have to say. He's a wushu expert. His default mode is doing spins and little blade tests. He's always working out. He's kind of a natural showoff."

"My Miek design originated from when we were tasked to come up with background gladiator characters to populate Sakaar," Tully Summers says. "I wanted to do something different from the many humanoid fighters we already had in the works, so I tried imagine how an alien with a body type not suited to combat could enter the arena. A caterpillar driving a bladed exoskeleton was the result. In my original version, the caterpillar was bright green and contrasted with his suit more. The green was toned down to make him less obvious, and to require a double take to realize what he was. There were some concerns that it was still too whimsical, and we almost did not present it. I'm glad we did, as they liked it enough to use him as Miek, Korg's sidekick!"

■ SUMMERS

■ SUMMERS

■ ORTIZ

▲ SUMMERS

▲ FRANCISCO

ORTIZ ▶

In addition to Korg and Miek, the catacombs are filled with myriad creatures ready to take their turn in the arena, helping further enrich the world of Sakaar. "Basically, we were given a ton of reference, and we all just kind of picked characters," Concept Artist Constantine Sekeris says. "We could see what kind of design language Jack Kirby had, and each artist chose which characters they liked and did their own spin of them. You want fans to recognize who it is, like if they have the comic from 1975 and go, 'Wow, that character, in that frame, is actually in the film in the background.' This is one of those things where Marvel has such a huge library of characters, it just fed into our concepts."

■ BRICLOT JOYNER ▶

▲ ORTIZ

◄ SUMMERS

"We went through a couple of iterations with the Sakaar warriors," Concept Artist Michael Kutsche says. "But I was mostly trying to emphasize that they are a wild mix of characters from different parts of the solar system, even if they were all bipedal. Though I had to be careful to not make them look too *Star Wars*-like."

■ KUTSCHE

"Some gladiators are digital with a few practical elements, some are just makeup, some are just completely digital characters, while others are a hybrid of practical and digital," Sekeris says. "These characters, they really allow you to have fun with their place in the film because you get a lot of comedic tonal moments in the film. It's always fun to kind of have these kinds of characters."

◄ SEKERIS

▲ FRANCISCO

▲ JOYNER

▲ FRANCISCO

▲► SUMMERS

■ DIAZ & PARK

■ PARK

Thor ushers in a whole new look when he enters the arena. Besides the obvious haircut, the God of Thunder's costume received some minor Sakaaran modifications. "We have kept the same cuirass going through different phases," Costume Designer Mayes C. Rubeo says. "For the gladiator look, they added pieces to him because Sakaar is a world of spoils, where all the debris lands. So they use that. They recycle all those elements, and they make all their very synthetic clothing. And that's the look we wanted for Thor. Kevin and Taika wanted him to have something, a very foreign object next to him on his shoulder, and another piece on his leg that is so foreign to what his costume typically is. On top of that, he has a tattoo from when they processed him as a prisoner. You will see him with this red tattoo that comes from his face to the neck and to his cuirass and his pants. It is just telling us this is a prisoner of Sakaar, and he's a contender."

■ PARK

"The biggest piece that I contributed for Thor's gladiator look was the helmet," Visual Development Supervisor Andy Park says. "Taika always said he wanted a helmet that mimics and gives the feeling of his classic Thor helmet, without actually being from Asgard. We came up with the whole idea of when Thor first puts it on, it doesn't look like his helmet, but then when he flips the winged ears over, it kind of does, even though it is clearly different. That was really fun to tackle, because as a comic-book fan, I always want to see Thor in his helmet, and we haven't seen that since the very first movie."

■ PARK

"The planet of Sakaar was completely based off of Jack Kirby," Park says. "It's wackier than a lot of things that we've done with the super-bright primary colors, and things that clash and don't seem to go well together, and shapes that are really bold and rudimentary in a lot of ways—and yet they work. I mean, that was what Jack Kirby was a master of doing. Taika really gravitated toward that look, so some of our earlier gladiator Thor designs reflected that aesthetic."

■ **FRANCISCO**

■ PARK

■ SZE

■ SZE

▲ MEINERDING

▲FUENTEBELLA

▲ KUTSCHE

▲ ORTIZ

▲ KUTSCHE

BRICLOT ▲▶

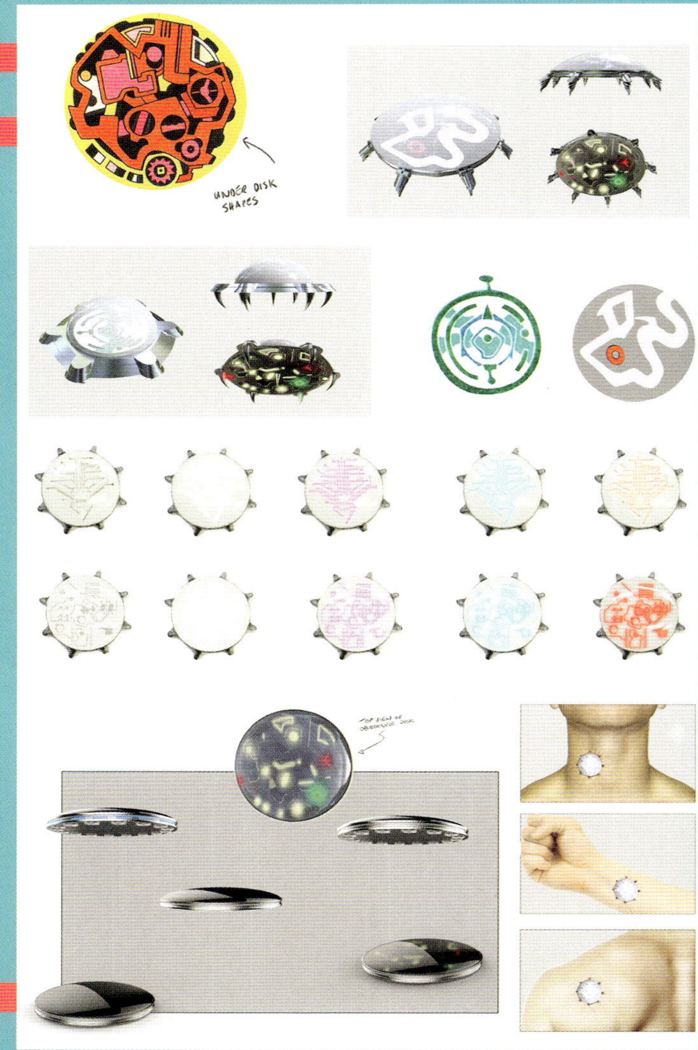

▲ BACALLADO

▲ SEKERIS

One of the many ideas borrowed from the comics is that of obedience disks: small circular objects used to control individuals. First appearing in the "Planet Hulk" storyline, these pieces of alien technology could bring even the strongest of fighters to their knees with the simple push of a button. "The obedience disks were surprisingly difficult, even though they are just supposed to be little disks that go on the warriors to kind of control them," Park says. "I think a big reason of why they were difficult is that nobody knew how prominent they needed to be, or what it was. Is it a circle? Is it not a circle? Does it have different colors on it? It can't look distracting—but it can't look like nothing, either. It ended up being fairly simple in the end, but sometimes you need to go through the entire design process of what it can be before you can settle on the correct design."

■ BRICLOT

110cm
A
B
C
D
THOR GLADIATOR SWORDS

SKULLS ON A STICK
THOR GLADIATOR MACE
ORTHO VIEWS

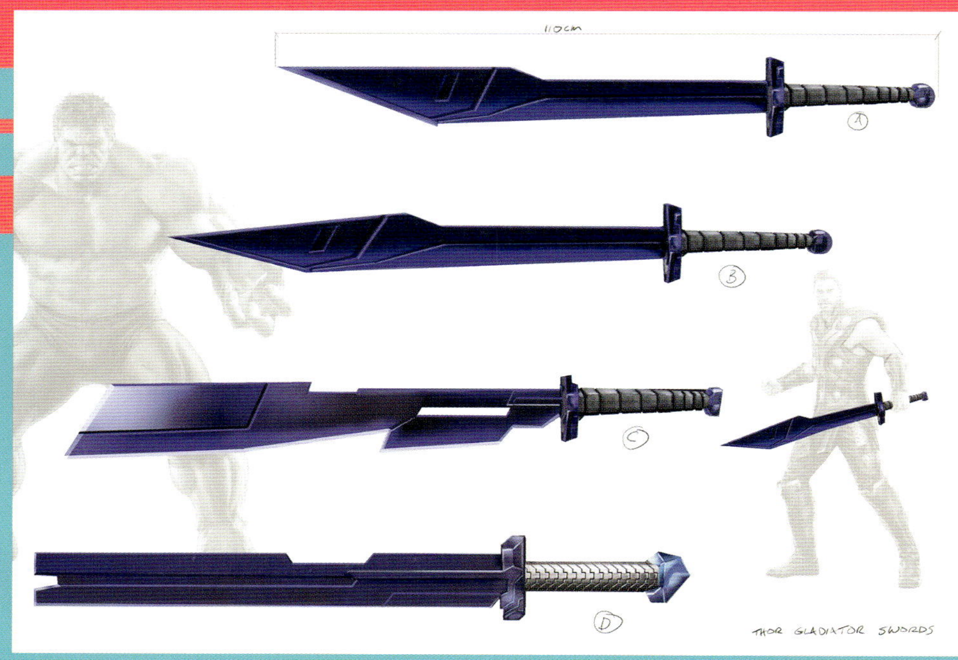

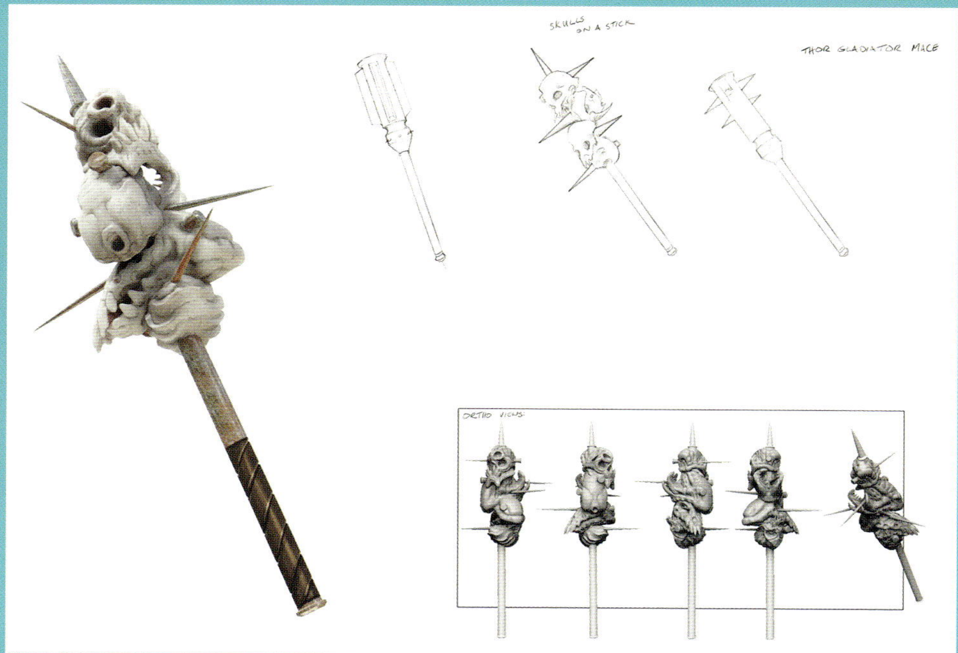

■ HEMPSON

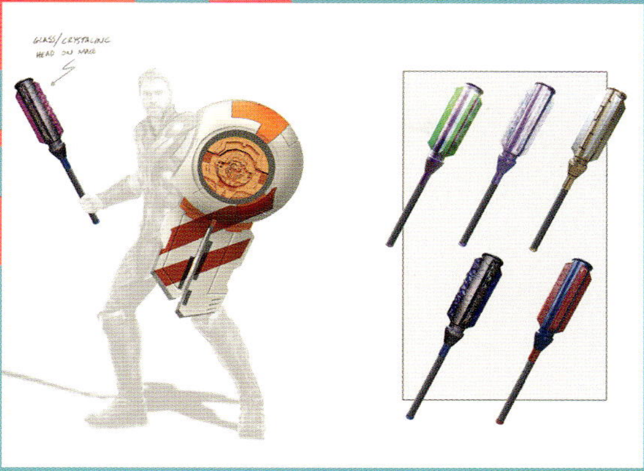

"Sakaaran in design, Thor's gladiator weapons were bright, colorful, anodized tools of death to entertain the masses in the arena," Hempson says. "I had the idea that Thor's swords could unfold in a futuristic way like a Swiss Army knife—that the blade could look as if it were broken when first unsheathed, then unfold along multiple blood gutters, becoming whole and deadly."

■ **BRICLOT**

▲ HARGREAVES

When two Avengers are poised to fight each other, not just any arena will do. Filmmakers were eager to ensure that this focal piece of Sakaaran architecture would be worthy of playing host to a battle wrought with such anticipation. "I think probably the first set that we really got our teeth into the concept was the Sakaar arena," Hennah says. "Taika's main thing was he didn't want it just to be another gladiatorial arena. We didn't want sandals and sand. We wanted something new and different and Sakaaran, Jack Kirby-ish. We did a number of passes on things like an arena with glass walls that you could look through and all sorts of wacky, weird, wonderful ideas, and then settled eventually on something that was more practical—which was to have an arena floor, but have 400,000 people in the bleachers around the arena."

◄ HEFFERNAN

■ PREVIOUS HARGREAVES

▲▼ HEFFERNAN

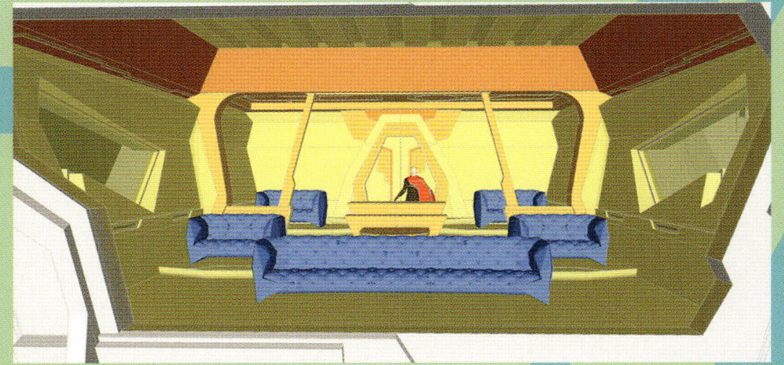

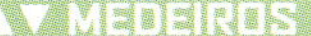

▲▼ MEDEIROS

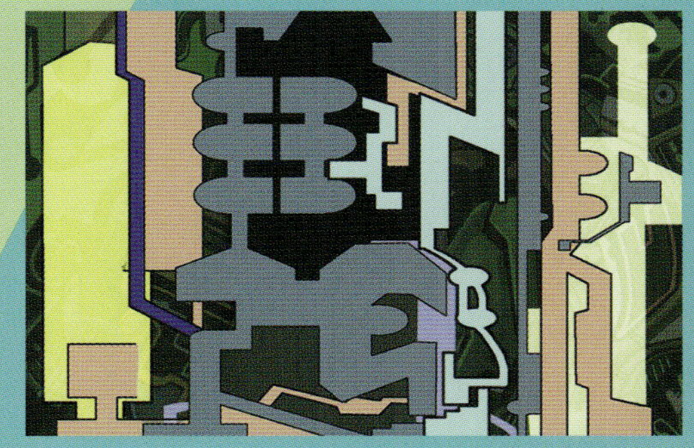

▲▼ HEFFERNAN

"Dan [Hennah] and I were in constant communication from the get-go," Rubeo says. "From the first day that we started to work, we had to start showing our stuff, crossing over with the color palette, crossing over with the styles. The result is what you see on the sets and costumes—they go so well together. Nothing clashes. It has to really be a complete harmony between me and the production designer because otherwise it's going to look like two different forces fighting. And we always avoid that."

■ RUIZ

■ BACALLADO

When Hair Designer Luca Vannella showed Taika Waititi a design he thought would be perfect for the Sakaaran servants, he had no idea what would happen next. "I showed a concept to Taika, and I said I'd really like to do something like this for the waitresses. I think it's simple, but intricate enough," Vannella says. "And he went, 'Well, what about if we do this—the same style at the back as the front so that when they come with a tray full of drinks, they look the same when they come and when they go.' I said, 'Oh my God, that's tricky. How can they see? How can they carry drinks? They can't see with the hair in front of the face.' Well, they did it, and they looked crazy. They looked amazing."

■ BACALLADO

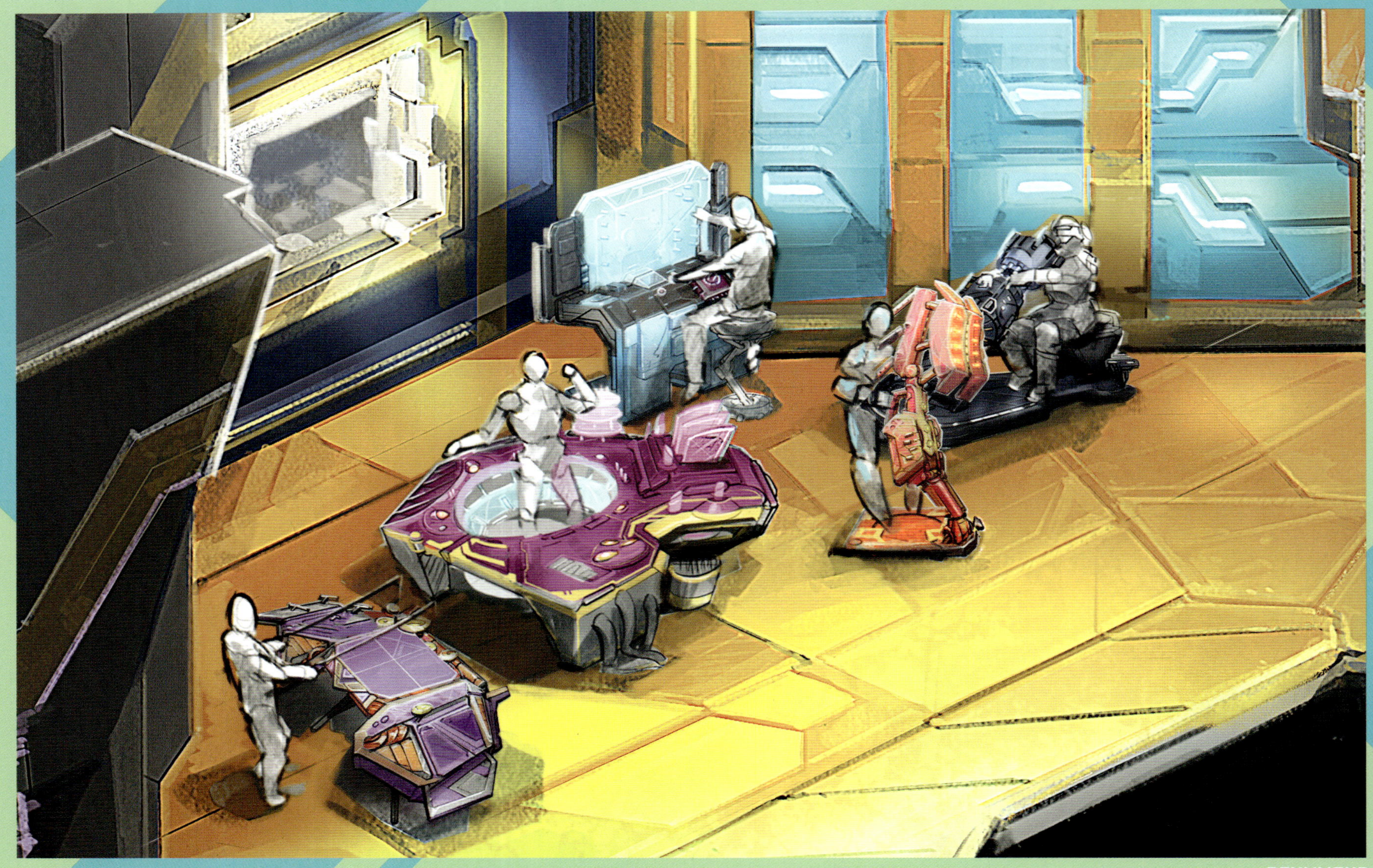

▲ DRUMMOND

Casting Jeff Goldblum as the Grandmaster offered the opportunity to add another element to the character's personality: a love of music. Goldblum, an avid pianist, was able to channel his experience performing with his band, the Mildred Snitzer Orchestra. "The Sakaaran musical instruments are pure Taika Waititi and Jeff Goldblum kind of waxing lyrical on Jeff Goldblum's character," Production Designer Ra Vincent says. "The Grandmaster is a lovable tyrant, and a talented one. So to give him his own band and obviously quite frightened band members was an inspired idea. The instruments that belonged with that concept were just as inspired.

"We fished around for conventional musical instruments that might be appropriate for Sakaar—but in the end, they really had to be from outer space. We ended up designing something like a full-bodied theremin, and a great big saxophone, and a very cool instrument that was reminiscent of a switchboard. The Grandmaster had two rainbow-colored pianos with Sakaaran keys, as there was only so much we could do design-wise to throw the traditional keyboard into a Sakaaran world. At the end of the day, Jeff Goldblum needed to play the piano, and we didn't really have time to reinvent the piano entirely. And then to have the chaos of 1,000 leads lying on the floor around the feet of the band—it's classic."

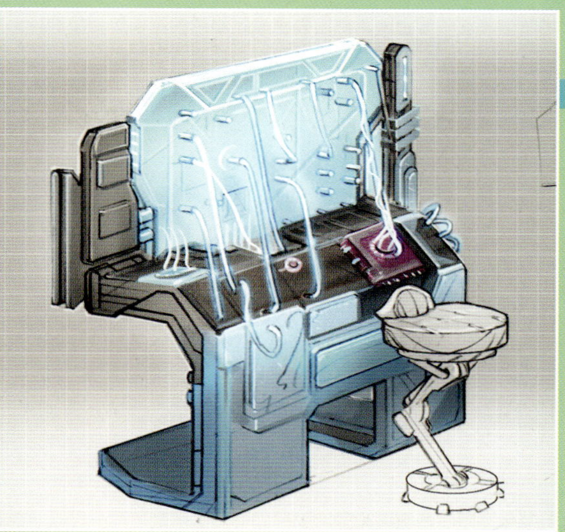

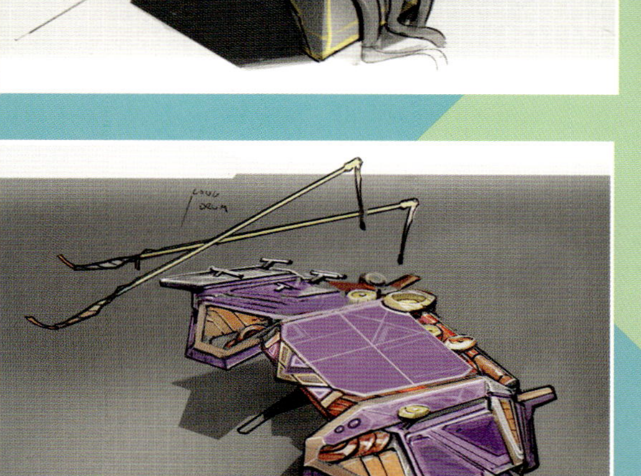

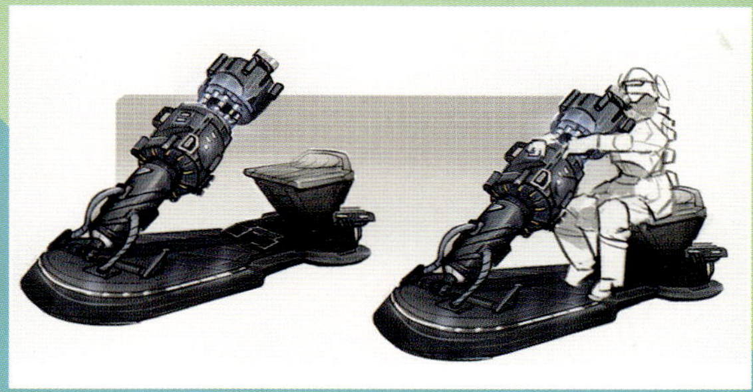

■ DRUMMOND

HULK

▲ MEINERDING
HEMPSON ►

◄▲ MEINERDING

ROSS ►

"When we meet the Hulk, he's not a guy who can easily turn back into Bruce Banner," Brad Winderbaum says. "He's a guy who's got both hands on the wheel of the car. And he's not giving the controls back to Bruce. We think a lot about what our characters' weaknesses are. And the Hulk's is Bruce. The one thing that scares this monster that can't be killed by any other beast he's fought is the idea that this little man is going to grab control of the car and take it away from him."

Since his last onscreen appearance in *Avengers: Age of Ultron*, the Hulk has become a gladiator on Sakaar. Designing a champion's look required artists to create a costume more intricate than a pair of purple cutoffs—a wardrobe befitting a warrior of his skill level and prestige. "The luxury of doing Hulk's gladiator armor is that as long as you do something that's reasonable, people will be excited to see it," Head of Visual Development Ryan Meinerding says. "We tried a couple of looks that were very closely related to what was seen in the 'Planet Hulk' comics, and for some reason, those weren't responded to—mostly because I think they knew they were going to go a little bit out there with Sakaar, so Hulk needed to reflect that. It was an interesting challenge to try to bring some of that crazy Kirby-ness into the armor for him, bringing in a lot of saturated color to the plume and to the other bits mixed in."

■ MEINERDING

■ MEINERDING

■ FRANCISCO

■ MEINERDING

"Doing a casual Hulk look—meaning he's not angry—was going to be interesting no matter what," Meinerding says. "And the comic reference given [from *Ultimate Wolverine vs. Hulk*] was very specific. We just tried to execute that as much and as specifically as possible."

■ **MEINERDING**

"Thor is basically a prisoner on Sakaar, and the Grandmaster offers him a deal and says, 'Look, you can win your freedom if you compete in these gladiatorial games and fight the champion, who's this reigning, unbeatable force,'" Chris Hemsworth says. "And Thor says, 'All right, well, point me in the direction. Where is he?' And he has no idea who it is or what it is, and then he's in the arena and out bursts the Incredible Hulk. And initially, Thor thinks, 'Oh, great, we're buddies. We know each other.' And Hulk kind of registers for a second, and then the berserker quality kicks in. And they go at it for a bit and beat the hell out of each other."

Hulk and Thor first fought in *Marvel's The Avengers*, and *Thor: Ragnarok* aims to notch up their clash in every way imaginable. "When it comes to this fight, how could you not be excited?" Storyboard Artist Todd Harris says. "Keeping character in this match was my biggest concern. It's more than just a big guy fighting a bigger guy. This could easily just turn into our heroes getting punched across the arena, then slowly getting back up while the other one runs over to get knocked back across the arena again, on and on. For me, skilled solider vs. brawler underpinned the approach to the fight. That conceit unfolds as weapons get removed and bare knuckles come into play, and how each of them takes advantage of those situations. Hulk to me is at his best with his hands free, and Thor is historically at his with a good weapon. Honestly, this fight could have been 90 minutes long. Both of them have so much personality and so many abilities, it would have been a blast—but we had a plot to think of."

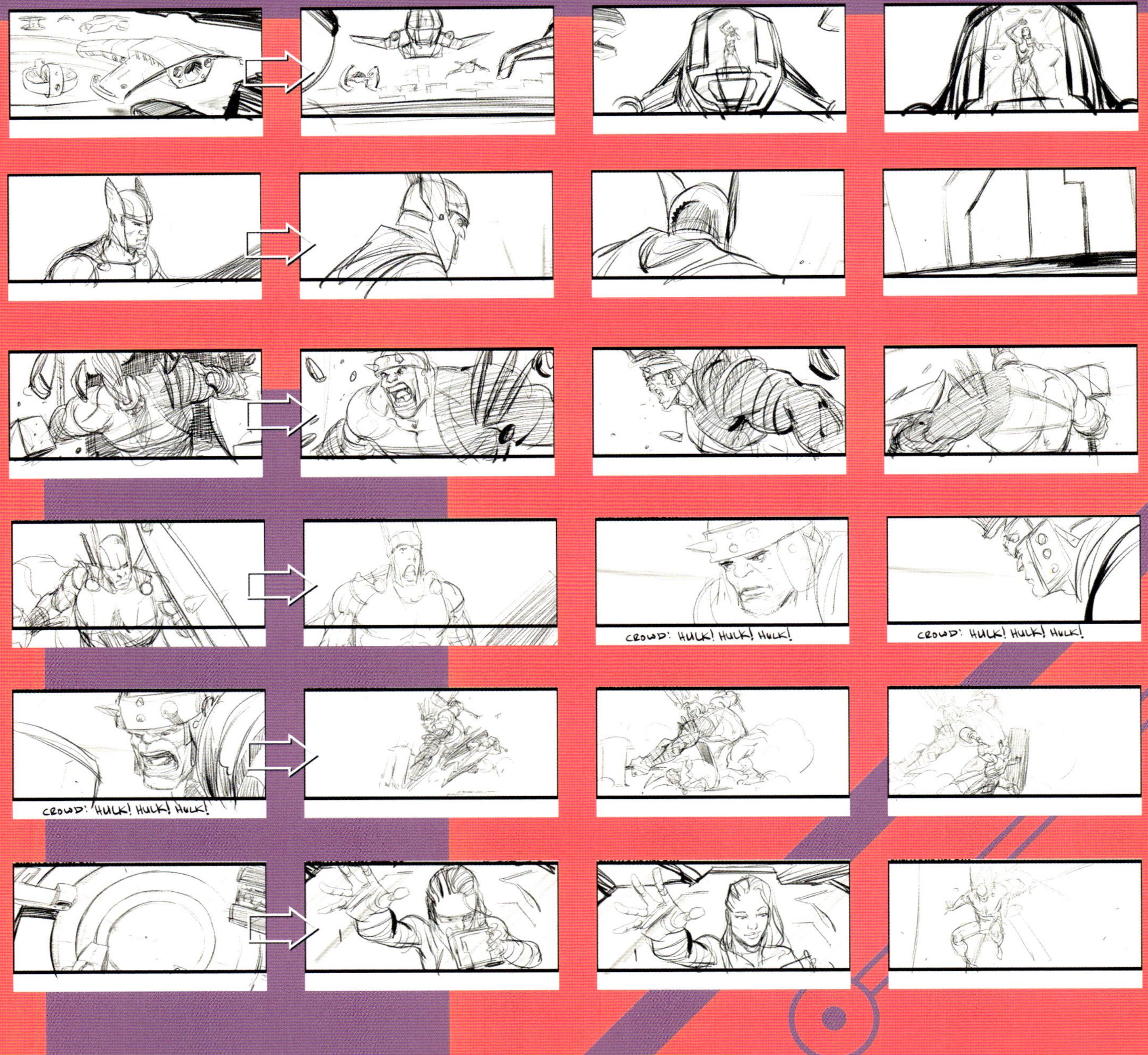

■ HARRIS

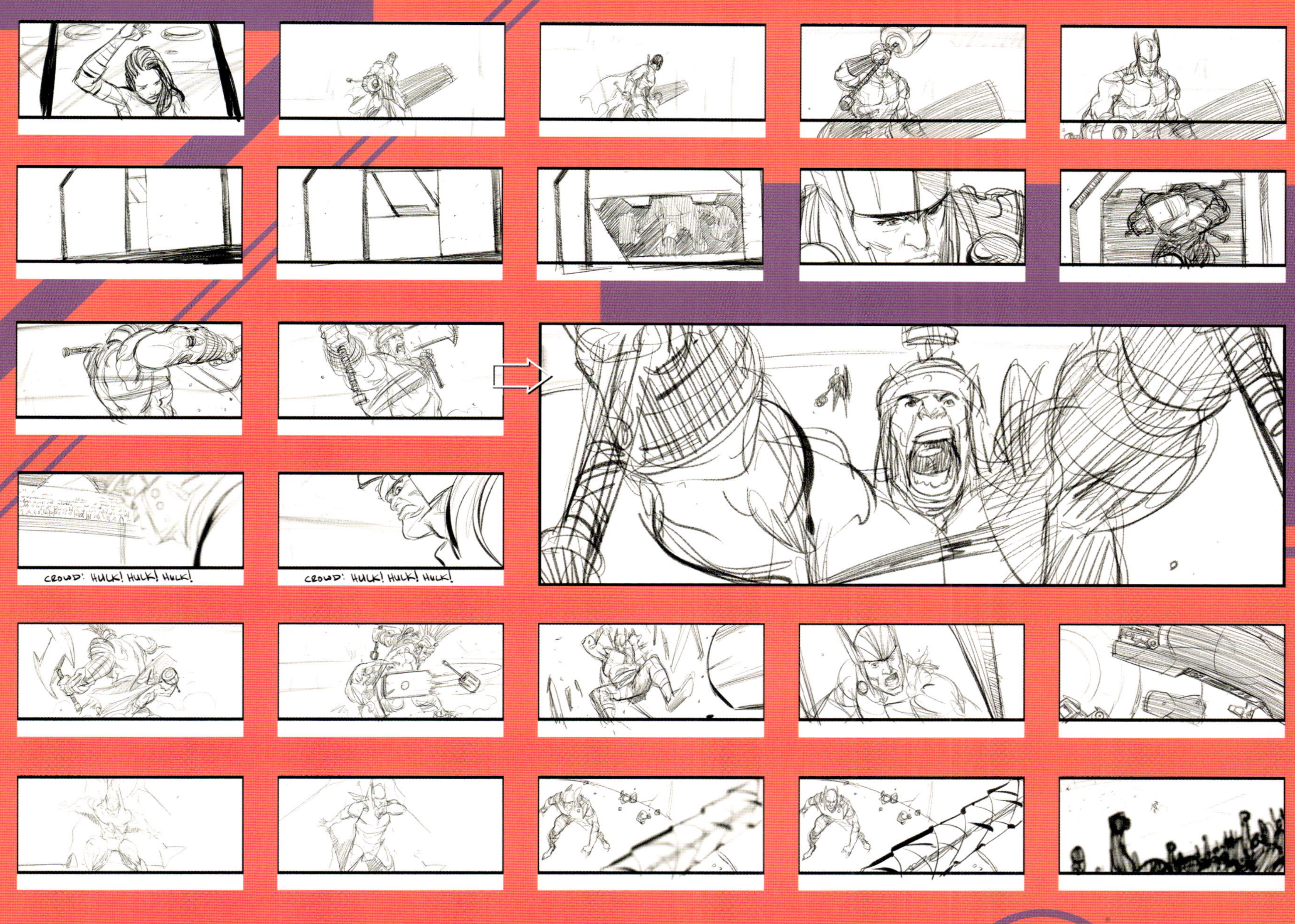
CROWD: HULK! HULK! HULK!
CROWD: HULK! HULK! HULK!

■ PARK

Losing is never easy. Having been bested by the Hulk in combat—with a little help from the Grandmaster—Thor awakens bruised and battered in the Hulk's private chambers. Realizing the green guy may be a powerful ally in the battle ahead, he tries to convince his friend to help him stop Hela back on Asgard. Easier said than done.

"[The Hulk] likes it on Sakaar," Executive Producer Brad Winderbaum says. "He's finally appreciated for what he is, which is a giant killing machine, which is why he makes such a great gladiator. Thor has to convince him to come with him. So how does he do that? He's going to haveto turn him back into Banner."

Even once he does, things remain complicated for our hero. "Banner describes to us that there's a pendulum effect," Winderbaum says. "He stayed so long in Hulk mode that now he's stuck in Banner mode. It's gonna take a lot to turn him back into Hulk. More than that, Banner doesn't want to turn into Hulk again. He feels like he's finally free from the Hulk, so he gets insulted when Thor implies that the only reason he needs him is because of the Hulk that lives inside of him.

"And even though he says the Hulk is buried deep within him, there are moments where you feel like the Hulk is going to erupt at any second with very little prompting—which puts a real strain on Thor, who's trying to sneak Banner across the city and off the planet without being discovered. He knows if Banner becomes the Hulk, they're screwed."

FROM SAKAAR

The Hulk is the champion, and to the victor go the spoils—in this case a massive suite in the Grandmaster's palace. "Taika's idea for the Hulk's suite was that it should be huge," Production Designer Dan Hennah says. "Hulk's big. It should be bigger. He's the favorite gladiator. He gets everything. So we went with huge. We went with our Sakaaran ideas, and we started working that up."

■ 224-227 **PARK**, 228-229 **BEN-MIMOUN** WITH **DEL RE**

RUIZ ■ ▶

▲ RUIZ

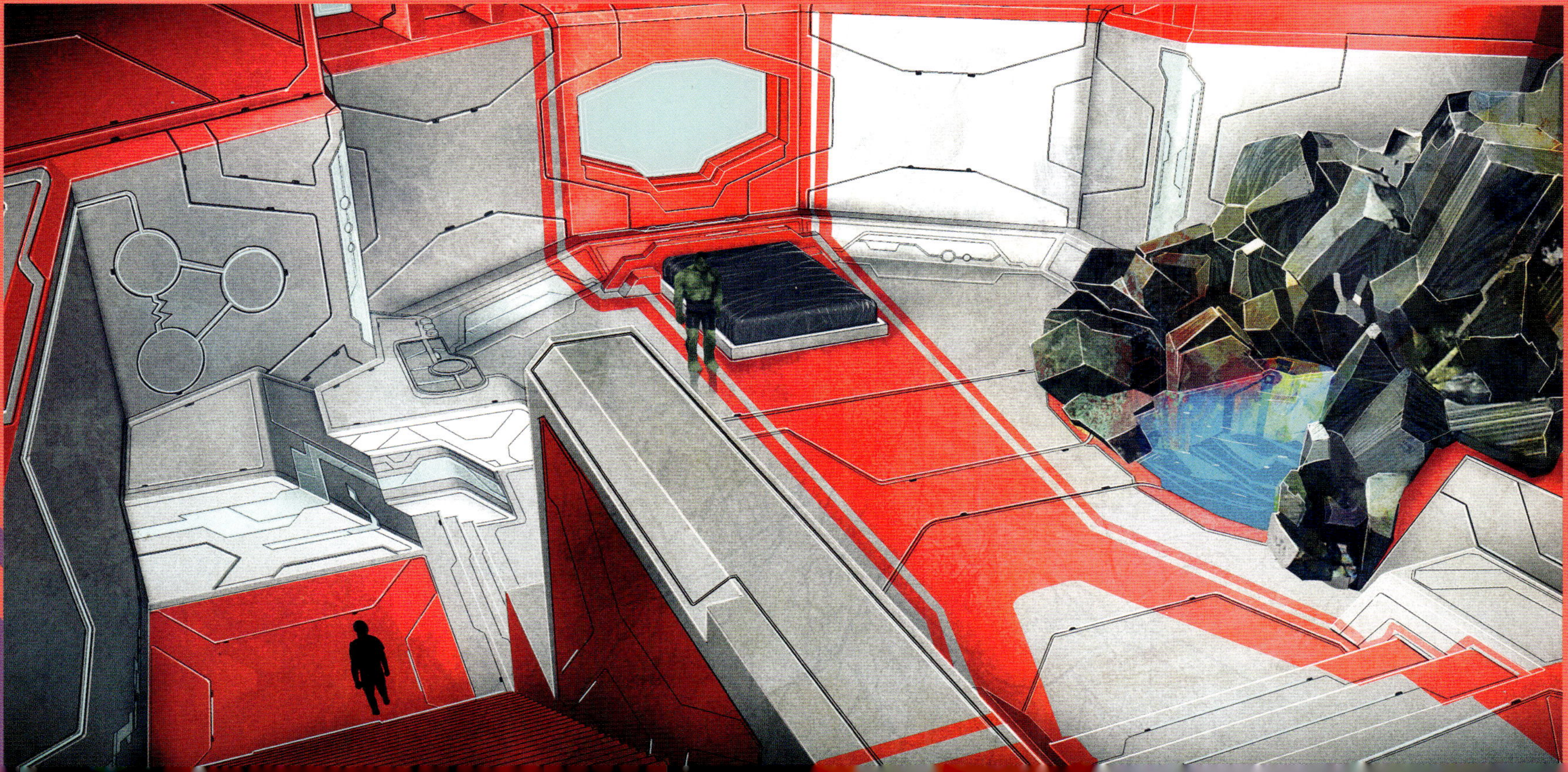

■ RUIZ

■ RUIZ

■ RUIZ

■ RUIZ

■ VINCENT

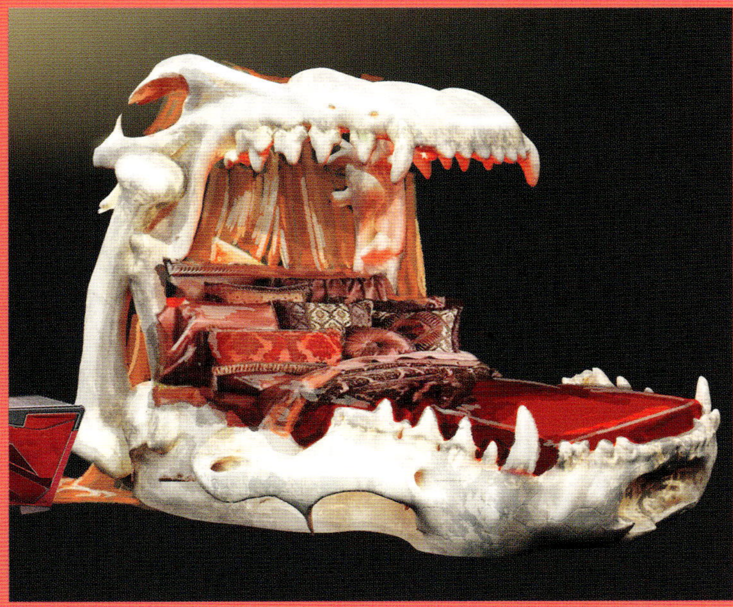

▲ VINCENT

The centerpiece of Hulk's massive suite is an equally massive bed, but it wasn't always that way. "We started off with a concept from Francisco Ruiz for Hulk's private chamber," Production Designer Ra Vincent says. "Back then, Hulk's den was more of a trophy room for a gladiator. And we talked with Francisco about various influences, and Hulk's character needing to feel like the ruler of his cave. So the first things that came to mind were the shields, the armor, and the bones of his victims all on display as trophies. And that inspired a throne. But then Hulk isn't one to be glorified and have to sit on a throne. He's a lot simpler than that; his character needed a more playful space. So the throne was replaced with something a little more modest, a little more domestic, and that was a bed.

"We initially set about offering up some pretty plain, pretty pedestrian versions of beds: a Hulk wood bed, a Hulk futon, and pelts and furs and cushions. There were many attempts before we actually decided that maybe we should come right back around to what we first thought, which was that Hulk needed a throne—or rather that there was something about the throne idea that was going to work for his bed. We thought perhaps that it could just be a giant skull. We know that the universe we're in has dragons, because we found one on Muspelheim, and obviously a planet like Sakaar has a lot of debris and creatures falling out of the sky—so perhaps one of Hulk's fallen victims was this giant dragon-esque creature.

"It happened that the best skull we could find for this was a weasel skull. We talked at length about how to break the skull open and how to put a mattress in it and stuff like that—but then, in true Taika fashion, he said, 'Why don't we turn it upside down?' And lo and behold, once you turn the weasel skull upside down and turn his jaw, it looks like a bed—which is just perfect, and fits with the playfulness of his character."

▲ HEFFERNAN

Finding harmony between the costumes and the sets on a colorful planet like Sakaar can be challenging, especially in crowd scenes involving hundreds of extras. "The new world will be a rainbow of colors," Costume Designer Mayes C. Rubeo says. "We will combine them with a very, very organized plan between the production designer and me. Costumes have to fit with the scenery. Otherwise, if you just throw many colors into another group of colors, it's a mess. So we actually are planning it very, very carefully."

"The final stroke is putting the population into the set," Hennah says. "And the costumes worked so well on those sets. Seeing that and the movement and the mass of people and the action taking place—that's why you go to all the effort, you know?"

◄ ▼ **BEN-MIMOUN**

◄ **HEFFERNAN**

■ PREVIOUS **BEN-MIMOUN**

▲ ALLAN

▲ ALLAN

◀ NOWAK ▲ HEFFERNAN ■ PREVIOUS NOWAK

▲ SZE

▲ HEFFERNAN

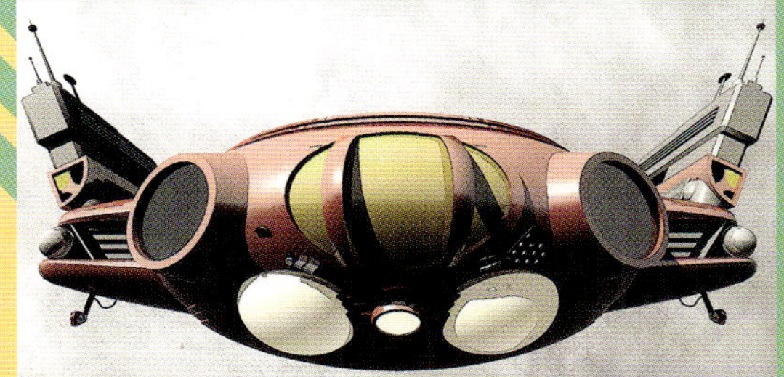

HARGREAVES ▶

"We've got flying bricks in the city; we have things that look like Skittles or Smarties that have wings on them," Visual Effects Supervisor Jake Morrison says. "It's all straight out of the Kirby artwork. It's absolutely crazy. And the challenge with that is to glue all these elements together and not make it look like you are in some insane album cover."

▲ RIHAL

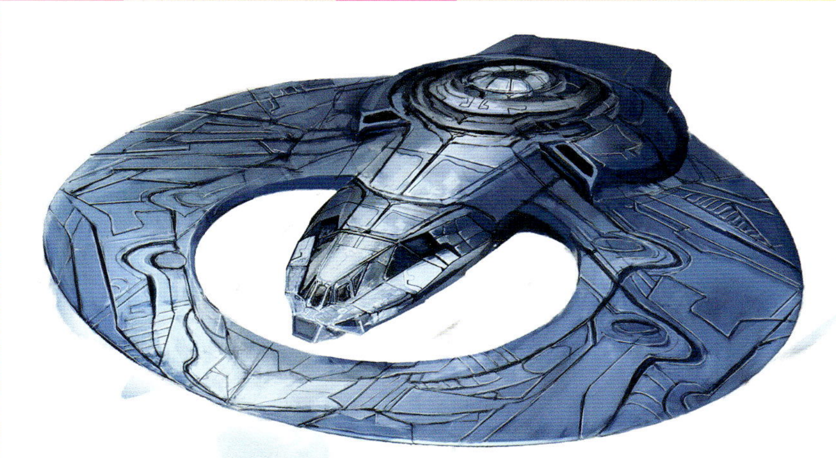

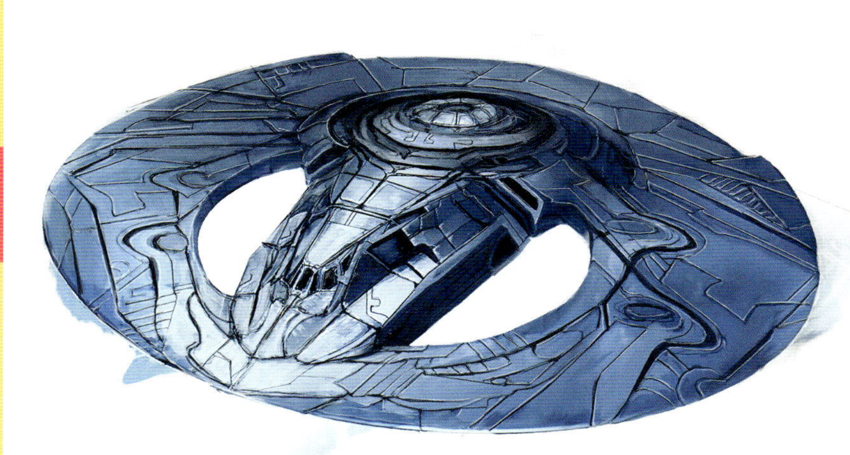

▲▼ HEFFERNAN

▲ NOWAK

■ PREVIOUS **ALLAN**

▼ ► **GRAY**

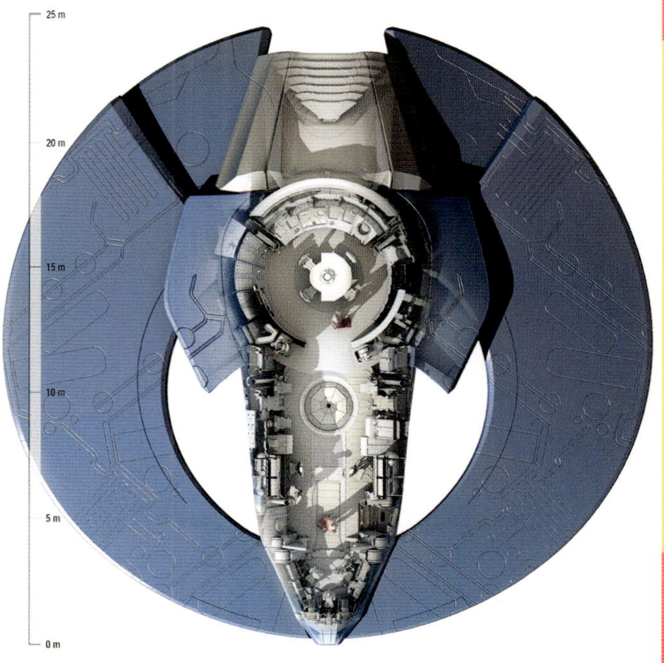

When our heroes formulate a plan to escape Sakaar by flying into a wormhole, the only piece of the puzzle missing is a ship strong enough to make the journey. Enter the *Commodore*. "The *Commodore* is the most extraordinary party bus," Morrison explains. "It's a spaceship, but it's not like one we've seen before. So we have the interior, which is incredible and cool and very decadent. And we get to build the exterior, which we see a great deal and get to put in some extreme stress situations. We have to take it through a wormhole, which takes us through this incredible debris field with all sorts of space junk, and then a few Easter eggs flying past. We get to find out how it flies. That's going to be one of the exciting things about getting into post. We get to design the engines. We get to flesh it out a little bit."

▲▼ RUIZ

▲▼ DONNELLY

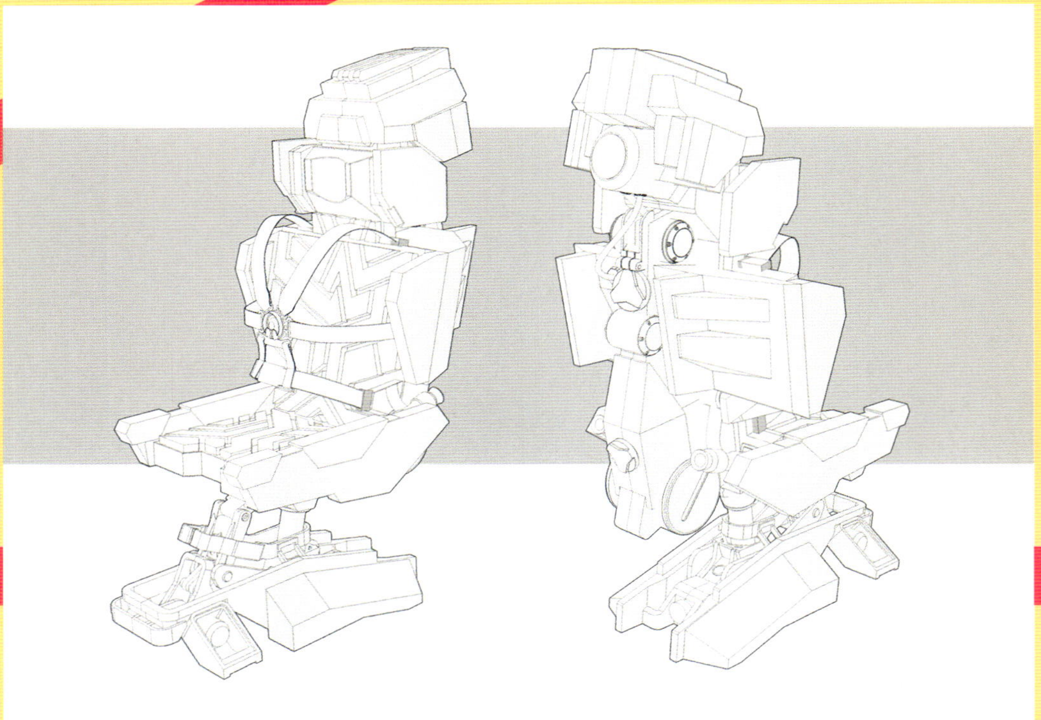

▲ DONNELLY

"The description and the writing for the *Commodore* is pretty suggestive in that the Grandmaster's private, pimped out wagon should be decorated as such," Vincent says. "Taika's aesthetic centerpiece and the references that he was giving us were classics like *Flash Gordon* and childhood memories of those fabulous old-school films with this very high-camp kind of party atmosphere.

"So for the *Commodore*, there was an opportunity to actually get down to extreme basics with a very stylish throwback to the '60s: shag carpet, orange velour on the walls, and stretchy rubber. We were fortunate in that we had a list of instructions from Taika about the mood we were going for. The end result felt like a Stanley Kubrick approach to *Flash Gordon*, but in a Taika Waititi kind of way. And the *Commodore* interior is kind of in another world of its own."

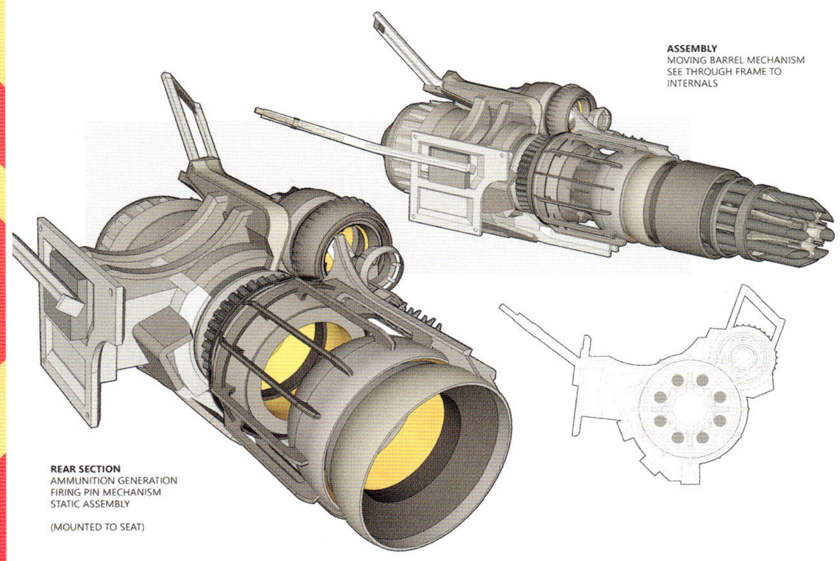

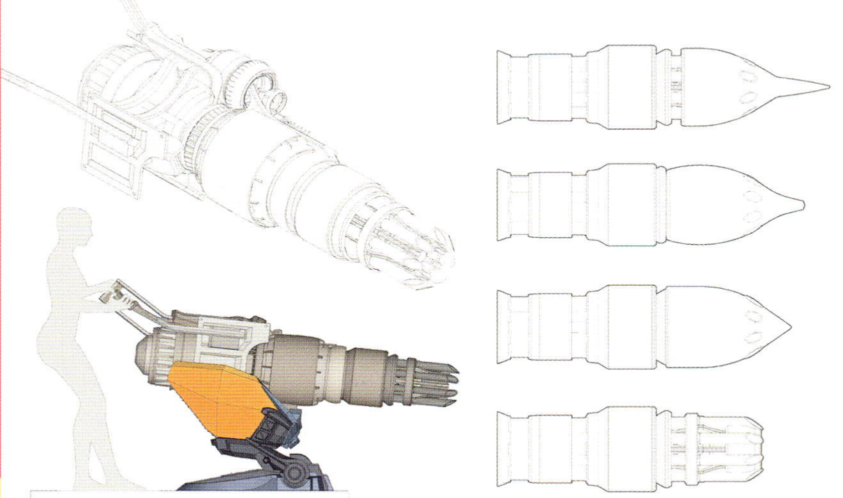

■ **DONNELLY**

"Once the *Commodore* had a structure, it was kind of easy to play out the different scenes in our minds and really spend time designing big-scope spaces within that one craft," Vincent says. "And as one of the ideas, I did a very quick character sketch of Valkyrie firing a cannon out of one of the open doors of the Commodore. It harkens back to *Tour of Duty* or *Rambo*, or one of those iconic young-boy moments where the hero is hanging out of the side of a helicopter with a machine gun taking out the bad dudes. That's the way that Valkyrie appeared to me in the *Commodore*."

VINCENT

"It's retro—it's the Grandmaster's party ship," Hennah says. "We worked on incorporating the Grandmaster's personality. And then during the process of designing, I found out that Jeff Goldblum was the Grandmaster. So we incorporated some of him into it, or some of how I perceived him."

■ RIHAL

▲ BEN-MIMOUN

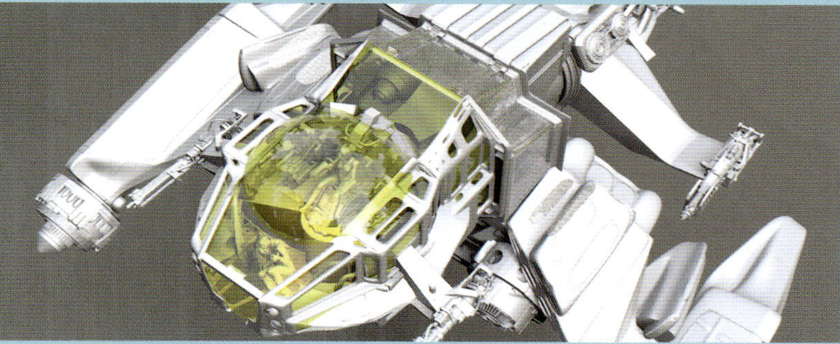

▲ BEN-MIMOUN

For this film, amazing and oddly designed spacecraft are the norm, and Valkyrie's ship is no exception. "*Warsong* was reverse engineered from a concept Dan Hennah and Taika Waititi had while talking together about this machine being something special," Vincent says. "And one of the very earliest ideas was that it was a gyroscopic capsule—the craft could perform amazing maneuvers, but then the driver would be encapsulated in a spherical cockpit that would always stay stabilized. So we could experience Valkyrie's slick driving skills from the exterior of the ship, while she's cool as a cucumber driving this maniacal rocketship through Sakaar and doing fabulous stunts. Apart from the splendid gyroscopic action that it does, it is also basically a machine gun on wings, and it's very effective as a scrapper vehicle for annihilating any opponents. So really, when you boil down the design process, it was, 'Okay, we need a ball, and then we need a housing for the ball, and then something to attach the guns to—and then, by the time we've done that, we ended up with a sphere, a couple of little wings with engines, and two massive cannons.' And that really designed itself. Then it was just tweaking the scale, and then assigning a really cool color scheme for it."

▲ BEN-MIMOUN

■ BEN-MIMOUN

■ BEN-MIMOUN

■ BEN-MIMOUN

Although dozens of wormholes funnel toward Sakaar, raining debris from throughout universe onto the planet's surface, only one can be used as an exit: the Magnitar wormhole. "The key point for us is trying to make sure that no matter how fantastical Sakaar looks and how sci-fi the whole thing goes, the wormholes have to look like funnels," Morrison says. "So when you see these things decked out in the sky, the audience has to be able to look and just in a second understand that this is a hole in the sky with a funnel above it. That has been our consistent brief for quite a while, just in terms of clear storytelling so people understand that this is a place where people end up. You cannot leave Sakaar. These funnels go down—they do not go up. And that's why the end of the second act is so key to create the Magnitar wormhole, which is the only one that you can escape out of—but is so horrendous, and is so incredibly destructive, that only a fool would ever attempt to fly a spaceship into it." Thankfully, Thor, Banner, and Valkyrie are just the team of "fools" crazy enough to attempt this. A sequence of high-flying action ensues as our heroes try to outrun the Grandmaster's pilots and ascend directly into the Magnitar wormhole to escape.

■ PREVIOUS **SZE** **MACKIE ▶**

BATTLE FOR ASGARD

Asgard has changed since Hela's arrival. The Goddess of Death has killed all Asgardian citizens who opposed her. As Hela slowly grows stronger, Heimdall, always one step ahead, has hidden as many Asgardians as possible away from her grasp, biding time until Thor returns.

When Thor finally arrives back home, he carries with him a cloud of doubt. Is he strong enough to destroy Hela? Is he smart enough? Can he do what is necessary to save his people? "On Sakaar, Thor is pushed to his absolute limits," Executive Producer Brad Winderbaum says. "He's lost his hammer, is tagged with a shock collar, has his iconic hair cut off, and has to use all of his wit and smarts to get off the planet. By the time he arrives on Asgard to face the most powerful being he's ever had to fight, he is completely exhausted and at the end of his rope. He knows that he doesn't have the strength to defeat Hela. But in the end, that's not what matters to him. What matters to him is saving the innocent people trapped on his homeworld. And he's willing to sacrifice everything to make sure they are safe."

HEIMDALL

"Heimdall's always been a very important character in the Thor movies," Executive Producer Brad Winderbaum says. "He's a very serious character. He mans the wall of Asgard. He's the first line of defense. And when we meet him in this film, he's in a very different place. He's been cast out. He was put on trial for treason because of the events of the second Thor movie and escaped, ran away, and is now living in the hills behind the city. And no one can find him because he has the power to see where anybody is at any time."

"When Heimdall was in charge of the observatory, he had to wear a very tough cuirass and armor because he was the man that was in charge of the opening and the closing of the Bifrost," Costume Designer Mayes C. Rubeo says. "And therefore, sending people in and out. He was in complete control of immigration, and a defense system of Asgard. But he had to leave. He was trying to stay alive, and his look is different now. It feels almost like he took vines and leathers from the place that he was around. His color is completely different. I wanted to keep colors to him that were more down to earth, almost Namibian. Really beautiful. You could see it in the mountains of Asgard. It is a concealing look. It isn't a show-off look."

◄ **DIAZ** ▲ **SZE** ■ PREVIOUS **CAMPBELL** WITH **DEL RE**

■ DIAZ

"Early on, the Asgardian refugees were hiding in a mountain cave with Heimdall, and this was an attempt to show how Hela could break it down," Concept Artist Jackson Sze says. "Using her powers, she could manifest solid shapes that could strike the rock face, and ultimately be powerful enough to bring down an entire mountainside."

■ PREVIOUS **SZE**

▲ **HEFFERNAN** **SZE** ►

▲ BRICLOT

ALLAN ▶

FENRIS

"Fenris is a mythical creature—part wolf, part dog—about 35 feet long," Visual Effects Supervisor Jake Morrison says. "He has smoldering green eyes similar to the D-Guards to keep it thematically correct. We have definitely gone into the full mythical realm for Fenris."

In early preproduction, concept artists explored other design options and angles for the four-legged fiend. "Fenris is a godly, powerful creature with the look of a wolf," Concept Artist Aleksi Briclot says. "A really big one. For some of my proposals, I stayed close to the shape of a classical wolf while making it slightly longer with a thinner waist and higher withers and a very defined muscular structure. Some scars on the muzzle and a blank eye help to show that he had seen a lot of battles before. Then we explored several crazier iterations, like one with a body made with Nordic interlace designs in motion, and one with a body like a black hole containing a whole universe close to exploding."

■ PREVIOUS **FRANCISCO**

▲▼ BRICLOT

▲ BRICLOT

▼ JOYNER

▲▼

▼

▼ KUTSCHE

▲▼BRICLOT

FRANCISCO ▶

▲ KUTSCHE

▲ ALLAN

▼ SHUI

"Hela believes that she should be the queen of Asgard, and that this is her palace," Executive Producer Victoria Alonso says. "So she is left with the emptiness of thinking that Asgard, what she needs to conquer, is a place, and forgets all about its people—and if you ask me, that's the key to any kingdom."

Thor: Ragnarok ventures beyond the main halls of Asgard to its back-alley streets and plazas, allowing the production team greater freedom to explore new ways of depicting the Nordic-inspired city. "I think it's like a Norse area on steroids, really," Production Designer Dan Hennah says. "It's stone, so it has a romantic sort of feel to it, but it's also Norse in that we use a lot of the shapes—the finials on buildings, the gold in the architecture, a lot of the decorative ropework, a lot of stonework, those sorts of things. We're not in the palace. We are actually in the back streets. We're trying to retain the formality of the sort of Asgard thats already been established, but also loosen it up a little bit into the other parts of town."

■ 284-285 **PARK**, 286-287 **FRANCISCO**

■ **HEFFERNAN**

▲ HEFFERNAN

▼ CAMPBELL

▼ ALLAN

◄ SERKERIS ▲ HEMPSON

"It was decided pretty late in the game that the filmmakers wanted Valkyrie to have a classic Asgardian costume as initially she was only going to get one look for the film," Visual Development Supervisor Andy Park says. "A lot of artists tackled the project and did versions of what they thought the classic Valkyrie design should be. They ultimately liked the silver-and-white look Constantine Sekeris created. It's really cool."

"Valkyrie's sword, Dragonfang, was influenced by some designs of early Asgardian weapons, from a period of time when Asgard was less peaceful," Concept Artist Jake Hempson says. "The sword uses some crueler shapes on the profile, harkening back to some of Loki's weaponry, but with a bleached-white hilt carved from the fang of a dragon and the bright blue-purple of the blade itself."

"The Valkyries are part of an elite force of Asgard," Park says. "They have always been something Marvel has wanted to include in the MCU. We had discussed using them before during the development of both *Thor* and *Thor: The Dark World*, but ultimately, they never felt right for inclusion. Now, for the first time, we actually get to use them in *Thor: Ragnarok*."

VALKYRIE

■ SEKERIS

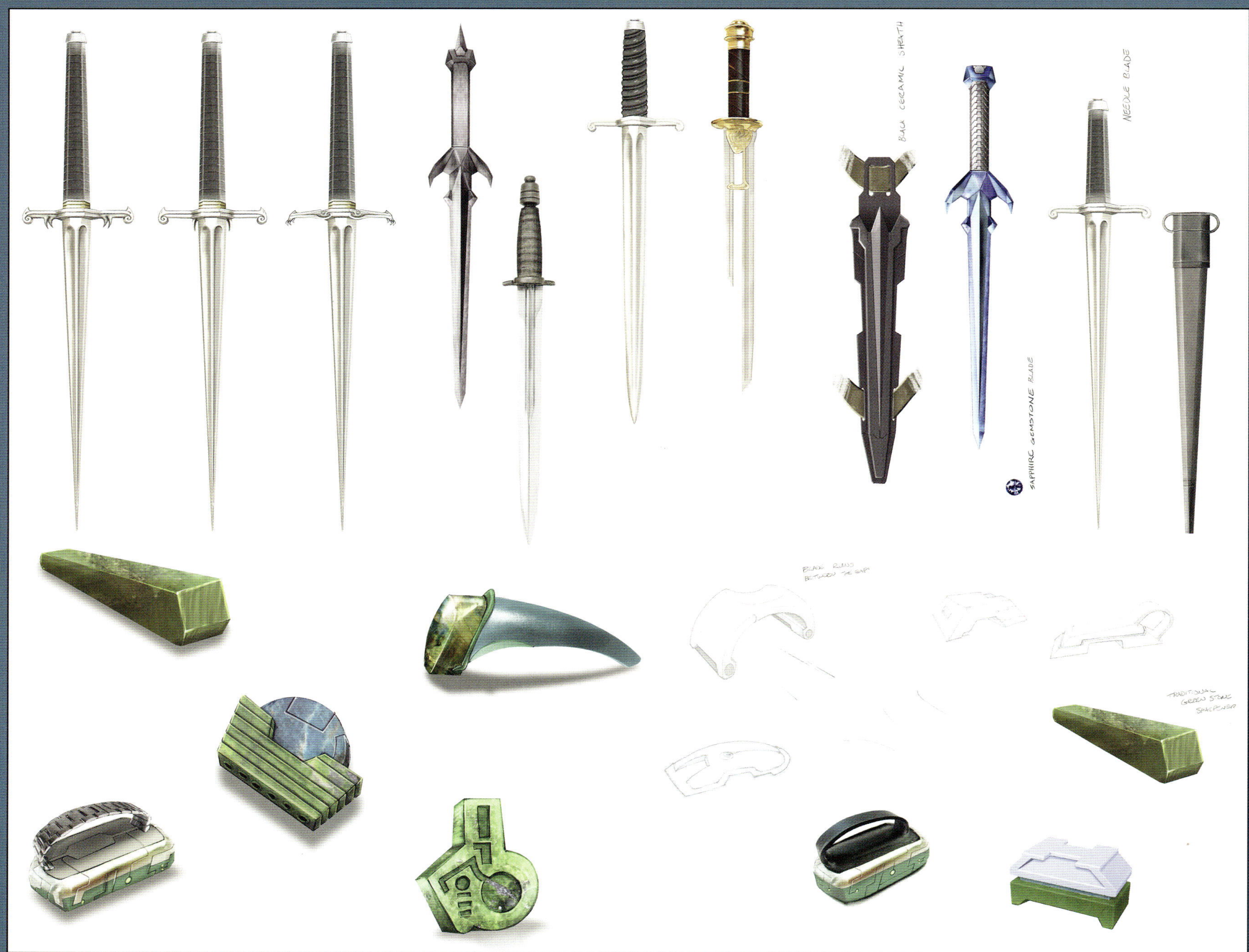

BLACK CERAMIC SHEATH
SAPPHIRE GEMSTONE BLADE
NEEDLE BLADE
BLADE RUNS BETWEEN THE GRIP
TRADITIONAL GREEN STONE SHARPENER

■ HEMPSON

▲ FRANCISCO

◄ BRICLOT ■ SUMMERS

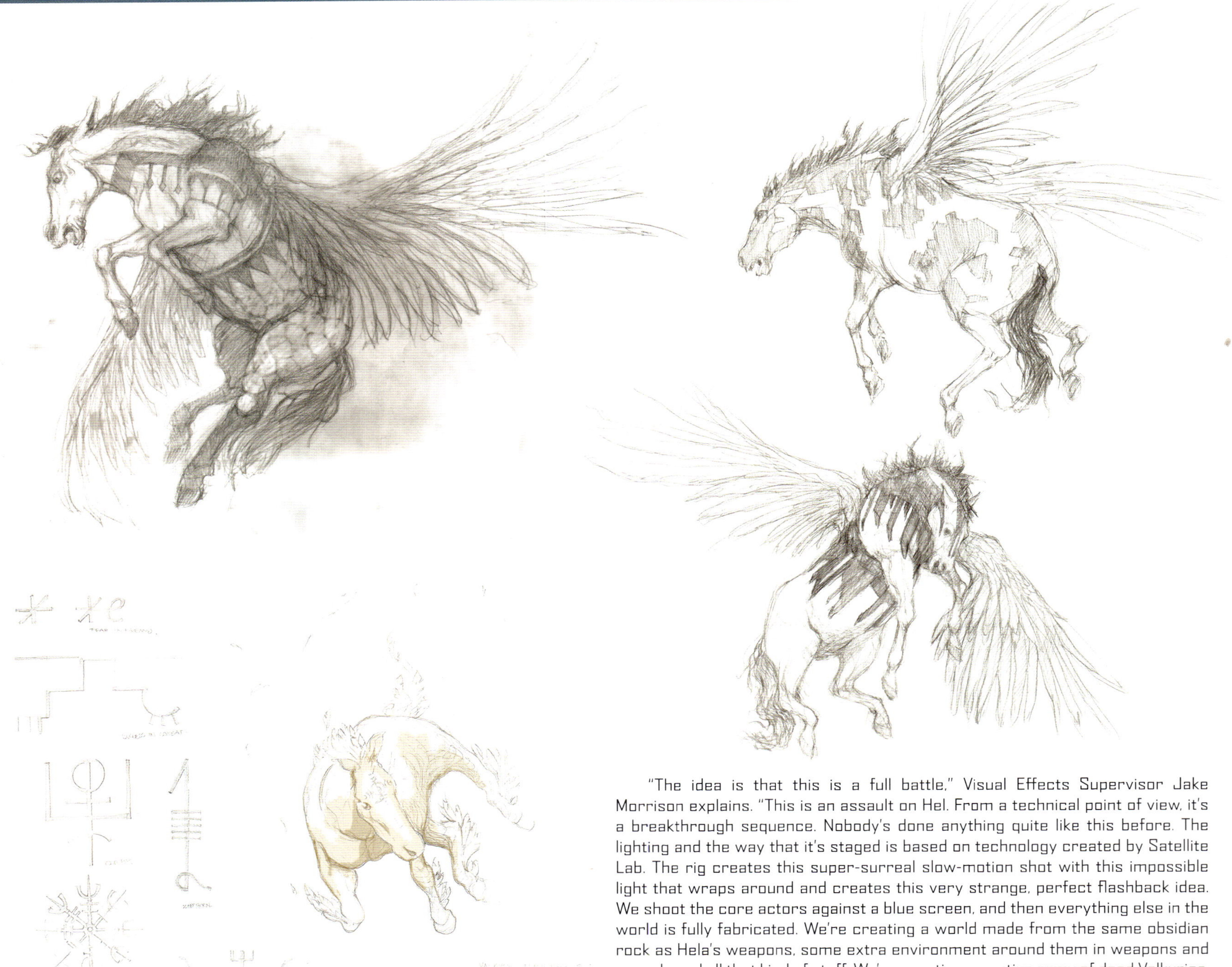

"The idea is that this is a full battle," Visual Effects Supervisor Jake Morrison explains. "This is an assault on Hel. From a technical point of view, it's a breakthrough sequence. Nobody's done anything quite like this before. The lighting and the way that it's staged is based on technology created by Satellite Lab. The rig creates this super-surreal slow-motion shot with this impossible light that wraps around and creates this very strange, perfect flashback idea. We shoot the core actors against a blue screen, and then everything else in the world is fully fabricated. We're creating a world made from the same obsidian rock as Hela's weapons, some extra environment around them in weapons and swords and all that kind of stuff. We're creating an entire army of dead Valkyries, plus some Valkyries that are not dead and are getting up and trying to attack Hela—and then, in the sky, we've got portals being created left, right, and center, and we also have dead winged horses that are dropping out of the sky."

■ PREVIOUS **PARK** ▲ **VINCENT** **CAMPBELL** ▶

"Kevin Feige specifically asked for this particular keyframe because he wanted to show it to Tom Hiddleston before they talked about *Thor: Ragnarok* and discussed what Loki was going to do this time around," Concept Artist Jackson Sze says. "I used Anthony Francisco's costume design for Loki. It was fun to do the character in a savior pose."

"Loki is willing to accept the possibility of being a hero," Tom Hiddleston says. "And I remember when I met with Kevin Feige in LA a month before we began shooting. I sat down with him across a table, and one of the first things he said was about my favorite moment in this film, Loki's return.

"Of course, Loki does it in the most grandiose, egomaniacal way—which is helmet on, cape on, arms outstretched, 'your savior is here.' But nevertheless, he does come and join the party, and I love that."

■ PREVIOUS **SZE** **SZE** ▶

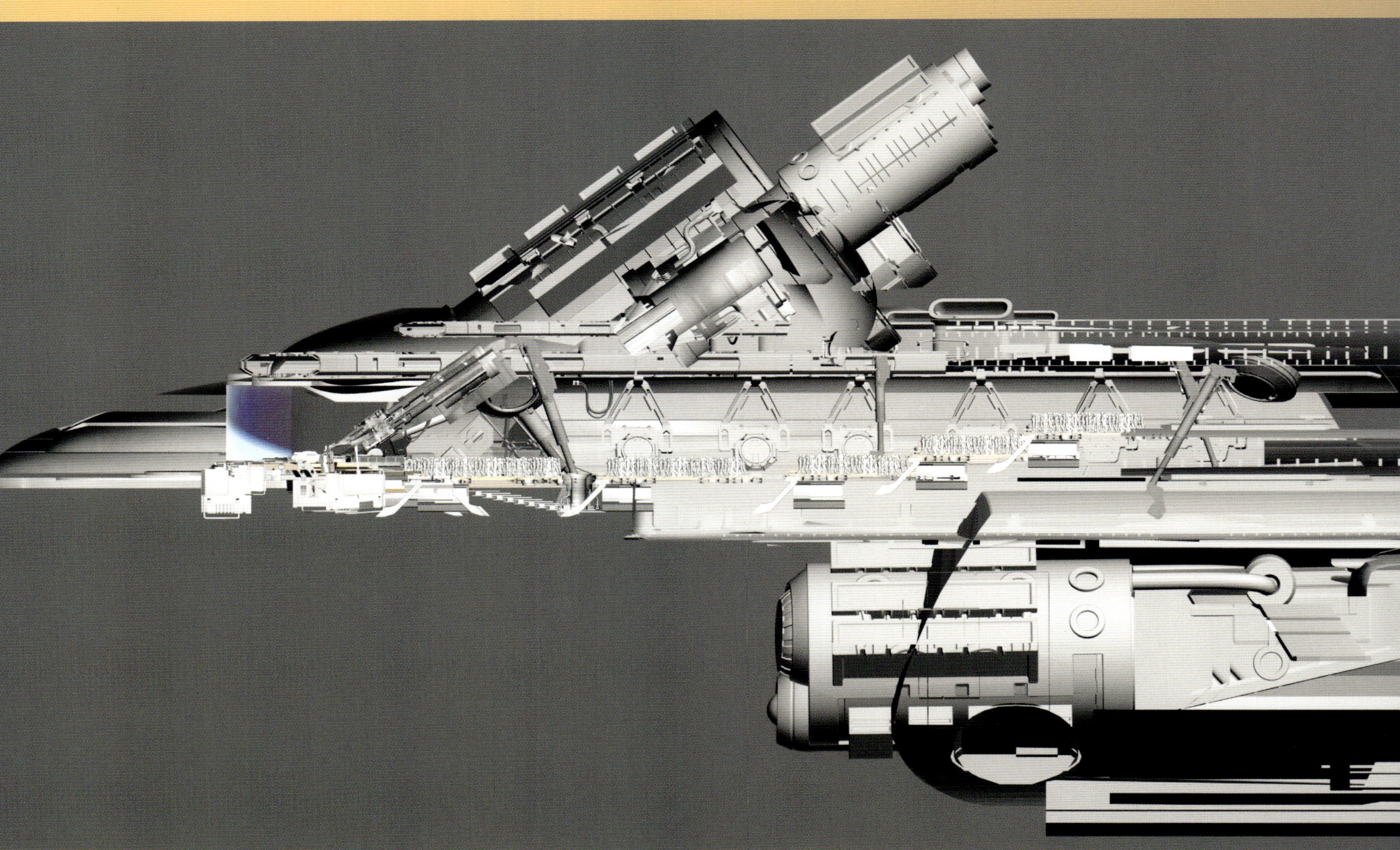

Not to be confused with the Dark Elf vessel of the same name, the *Ark* was more a nod to the biblical Noah. "The Ark is actually a massive Sakaaran ship called the *Statesman* that Loki and the gladiators steal from the Grandmaster's private garage," Executive Producer Brad Winderbaum says.

"The architecture of the ship is familiar to Sakaar and Grandmaster design," Production Designer Ra Vincent says. "And like the arena, the greatest amount of attention is focused on the building style of the Sakaaran dictator."

■ 304-305 **SZE**, 306-307 **KUTSCHE**

▲► **NOWAK**

◄ BRICLOT

▲ FUENTEBELLA

"I think that this film is very different," Alonso says. "It's different in every way that we have done this except for the very similar theme of friendship and family that we continue to share and to discover in our movies. We get to see Thor in a very different light as a man who has to rediscover who he is. That journey is really fun. He's very, very funny and light. There's a freshness about him that is different from the other two movies, and I think a lot has to do with the banter with Valkyrie and Bruce Banner in addition to the fully established banter with Loki. The performances are just so solid throughout the movie, and to have Chris Hemsworth be standing side by side with the amazing Academy Award-winning Cate Blanchett is a beautiful thing. We are honored to have them all."

■ 312-317 **SZE** **BRICLOT** ▶

AFTERWORD 2017

by ANDY PARK

I grew up in the '80s watching cartoons and singing commercial jingles. I read comic books and dreamed of drawing them one day. I was a kid who loved being a kid. I didn't want to grow up, and I gotta confess, that's kind of been my mantra throughout my life.

Don't get me wrong—I've embraced the challenges and responsibilities of adulthood, but I also have never wanted to lose that childlike quality that tends to get buried under the rigors of life as we get older.

My career has reflected this desire to not want to "grow up." I started out my career drawing "funny books"—or as most people know them, comic books. I drew the adventures of Lara Croft and the visceral battles of Wolverine on titles such as *Tomb Raider* and *Uncanny X-Men*. I then became a concept artist designing mythological heroes and fantastical beasts for the Sony PlayStation video-game franchise *God of War*. And my latest adventure has been designing action heroes (and villains) for the big screen here at Marvel Studios for over seven years. It truly has been a dream come true for both the kid and adult in me.

Thor: Ragnarok embraces the kid in all of us while never forgetting the realities that face our heroes. It's the end of days, and the entirety of Asgard's existence hangs in the balance. And even through these direst of circumstances, this movie never lets us forget that we, the audience, are here to have fun. We want excitement—to cheer, laugh, and cry. This is the genius of Taika Waititi.

If you've seen any of Taika's movies, you know he gets it. He's never going to take himself too seriously. But he also never neglects real life and real people. It is this type of director that Kevin Feige, Louis D'Esposito, and Victoria Alonso have been so good at bringing onto our team. They get it, too. It's not just about a résumé. It's about talent, potential, and vision—and a uniqueness in vision.

I had the honor of leading the Visual Development team on this film. Starting with Taika's direction (oftentimes a sketch, since he's a great artist himself) to working with all my artists, it was one of the best experiences in all my years at Marvel. I loved the risk that Taika and Marvel Studios have taken with this third iteration of the Thor story. It's the same thinking they had when tackling *Captain America: The Winter Soldier* and the then-obscure franchise *Guardians of the Galaxy*. There was a bold choice to go in a different direction that didn't completely make sense yet completely did. It's a bit scary—but again, I find that our best movies tend to be the ones where we are a bit scared. That means that we're not just playing it safe.

This is a bold new Thor. When you take away the thing that is so signature to who he is and what makes him cool—his hammer (not to mention his long hair)—you are telling the audience that we're shaking things up. How do you make Thor cool without his magical hammer, Mjolnir? This movie will show you. He's the God of Thunder, not the God of Hammers (and long hair).

Thank you first and foremost to our fearless leaders, Kevin Feige, Louis D'Esposito, and Victoria Alonso. I love working for a company where I have the utmost trust in the leadership. They truly get it, and the unprecedented success of Marvel Studios is squarely credited to these three amazing leaders. The producer on this film, Brad Winderbaum, was such a great collaborator to work with. I appreciated his positivity and confidence in me. He was a great leader as well. Costume Designer Mayes C. Rubeo embraced the challenge and scope of this type of film that helped make every character stand out on his or her own and still remain cohesively connected. This film was definitely pushing the boundaries when it came to the visuals, and Mayes certainly delivered. Production Designers Dan Hennah and Ra Vincent created magic. Creating the look of Sakaar, with all its crazy colors and shapes, was not an easy task to accomplish, but Dan and Ra have created a world that is so unique and reflects the reality of what Jack Kirby had created in a 2D format so many decades ago. It's truly some amazing work. And Visual Effects Supervisor Jake Morrison truly is a wizard. He makes everyone look good. He creates what is not there and does it seamlessly. I appreciate Jake's generosity in our collaboration. It truly was a pleasure to work with him.

Then there's my department, the Visual Development department. Head of Visual Development Ryan Meinerding created the look of Hulk on this film, and he created yet another iconic look on top of his already long resume of iconic designs in the Marvel Cinematic Universe. He's an inspiration to us all. Thanks to AJ Vargas, our manager, and Bojan Vucicevic, our coordinator, for their ongoing support and professionalism. These guys are top notch and help make this department run as smooth as rain. And then there's the rest of the Visual Development artists who worked on this film: Jackson Sze, Anthony Francisco, Adam Ross, Ian Joyner, Tully Summers, Aleksi Briclot, Constantine Sekeris, Jerad Marantz, Karla Ortiz, and Michael Kutsche. Thank you for all your hard work, tireless hours, creativity, and dedication. You made my job not only easy, but also a pleasure. I'd work with these guys any day of the week. They're the best in the business.

Thor: Ragnarok is a game changing type of movie for Marvel Studios. It's not back to status quo at the end of the film. It's a complete film and yet makes you so anxious to see what will happen next. That's the magic of the MCU. It's exactly how I felt reading Marvel Comics back in my youth. So thank you, Marvel Studios, for allowing all of us to never fully "grow up."

ANDY PARK

CONTRIBUTOR BIOS 2017

DIRECTOR TAIKA WAITITI has carved out a diverse and highly successful career in his homeland of New Zealand as an Oscar-nominated film director, writer, painter, comedian, and actor. He has directed the two highest-grossing native feature-film releases in New Zealand history: *Boy* (2010) and his most recent release, *Hunt for the Wilderpeople* (2016). After attending Victoria University in Wellington, Waititi garnered a New Zealand Film Awards Best Actor nomination for his first acting role, that of the lothario flatmate in *Scarfies*. He next appeared in 13 episodes of the Kiwi TV series *The Strip* and the road movie *Snakeskin*. He next moved behind the camera, writing and directing the comedy short *John & Pogo* in 2002. His talent for character and story again earned him acclaim and awards recognition for his first feature-length production, *Eagle vs. Shark* (2007). Waititi was named Best Director by the New Zealand Film and TV Awards society (with two additional nominations for Best Picture and Best Screenplay) and earned a Grand Jury Prize nomination at that year's Sundance Film Festival. Waititi's second feature, *Boy* (which he not only starred in, but also directed and wrote), explores characters and ideas he introduced in his short *Two Cars, One Night*. The film was one of only 14 titles to make it into Sundance's World Cinema section in 2010. Waititi went on to direct several episodes of HBO's popular, Emmy-nominated comedy series *The Flight of the Conchords*, which starred another Kiwi native, Jemaine Clement. The pair won their homeland's second-highest comedy honor, a Billy T. Award, for their work together. Several years later, Waititi and Clement reteamed as co-directors, co-writers, and co-stars of the 2015 vampire comedy *What We Do in the Shadows*. The film collected dozens of global film awards and nominations, including the Midnight Madness/People's Choice Award at the Toronto International Film Festival; Best Original Screenplay from the San Diego Film Critics; and a Saturn Award nomination for Best Horror Film from the Academy of Science Fiction, Fantasy and Horror. Like his two previous features, the film had its world premiere at the Sundance Film Festival. In addition to casting himself in several of his own projects, Waititi (named as one of ten new talents to watch in the influential entertainment trade magazine *Variety* in 2010) made his Hollywood motion-picture debut in 2011 in *Green Lantern*, based on the iconic DC Comics character, portrayed in the film by Ryan Reynolds, and appears in *Thor: Ragnarok* as the effortlessly charismatic Korg.

Over the past decade, **PRODUCER AND MARVEL STUDIOS PRESIDENT KEVIN FEIGE** has played an instrumental role in a string of blockbuster feature films adapted from the pages of Marvel comic books. In his current role, Feige oversees all creative aspects of the company's feature film and home entertainment activities. He is producing such projects as *Spider-Man: Homecoming* and *Thor: Ragnarok* (both 2017); *Black Panther*, *Avengers: Infinity War*, and *Ant-Man and the Wasp*, which will be released in 2018; and *Captain Marvel* and the fourth Avengers film, which will be in theaters in 2019. Earlier this year, he produced *Guardians of the Galaxy Vol. 2*. In 2016, Feige produced *Captain America: Civil War*, which crossed $1 billion in global box office and was the year's highest grossing film, and *Doctor Strange*, which grossed more than $600 million worldwide. His previous producing credits for Marvel include *Iron Man 3*, *Marvel's The Avengers*, *Ant-Man*, *Avengers: Age of Ultron*, *Guardians of the Galaxy*, *Captain America: The Winter Soldier*, *Thor: The Dark World*, *Thor*, *Captain America: The First Avenger*, *Iron Man 2*, and *Iron Man*.

EXECUTIVE PRODUCER AND MARVEL STUDIOS CO-PRESIDENT LOUIS D'ESPOSITO served as executive producer on the blockbuster hits *Iron Man*, *Iron Man 2*, *Thor*, *Captain America: The First Avenger*, *Marvel's The Avengers*, *Iron Man 3*, *Thor: The Dark World*, *Captain America: The Winter Soldier*, *Guardians of the Galaxy*, *Avengers: Age of Ultron*, *Ant-Man*, *Captain America: Civil War*, *Doctor Strange*, *Guardians of the Galaxy Vol. 2*, *Spider-Man: Homecoming*, and *Thor: Ragnarok*. He is currently working on the highly anticipated films *Black Panther*, *Ant-Man and the Wasp*, *Captain Marvel*, and *Avengers: Infinity War*, as well as collaborating with Marvel Studios President Kevin Feige to build the future Marvel slate. As Marvel Studios co-president and executive producer on all Marvel films, D'Esposito balances running the studio with overseeing each film from its development stage to distribution. In addition to executive-producing Marvel Studios' films, D'Esposito directed the Marvel One-Shot *Item 47*, which made its debut to fans at the 2012 San Diego Comic-Con International and was featured again at the LA Shorts Fest in September 2012. The project was released as an added feature on the *Marvel's The Avengers* Blu-ray disc. D'Esposito also directed the second Marvel One-Shot *Agent Carter*, starring Hayley Atwell, which premiered at the 2013 San Diego Comic-Con to critical praise from press and fans, and is an added feature on the *Iron Man 3* Blu-ray disc. The One-Shot's popularity led to development of the TV series *Marvel's Agent Carter*. D'Esposito began his tenure at Marvel Studios in 2006. Prior to Marvel, D'Esposito's executive-producing credits include the 2006 hit film *The Pursuit of Happyness*, starring Will Smith; *Zathura: A Space Adventure*; and the 2003 hit *S.W.A.T.*, starring Samuel L. Jackson and Colin Farrell.

Marvel Studios **EXECUTIVE VICE PRESIDENT OF PHYSICAL PRODUCTION VICTORIA ALONSO** is executive-producing Taika Waititi's *Thor: Ragnarok*. In her executive role, she oversees postproduction and visual effects for the studio slate. She executive-produced James Gunn's *Guardians of the Galaxy Vol. 2*, Scott Derrickson's *Doctor Strange*, Joe and Anthony Russo's *Captain America: Civil War*, Peyton Reed's *Ant-Man*, Joss Whedon's *Avengers: Age of Ultron*, James Gunn's *Guardians of the Galaxy*, Joe and Anthony Russo's *Captain America: The Winter Soldier*, Alan Taylor's *Thor: The Dark World*, Shane Black's *Iron Man 3*, Joss Whedon's *Marvel's The Avengers*, and Jon Watts' *Spider-Man: Homecoming*. She co-produced Jon Favreau's *Iron Man* and *Iron Man 2*, Kenneth Branagh's *Thor*, and Joe Johnston's *Captain America: The First Avenger*. Alonso's career began at the nascency of the visual-effects industry, when she served as a commercial VFX producer. From there, she VFX-produced numerous feature films, working with such directors as Ridley Scott (*Kingdom of Heaven*), Tim Burton (*Big Fish*), and Andrew Adamson (*Shrek*), to name a few. In 2015, Alonso was an honoree of the New York Women in Film & Television's Muse Award for Outstanding Vision and Achievement. In January 2017, she received the Advanced Imaging Society's Harold Lloyd Award.

BRAD WINDERBAUM, VICE PRESIDENT, PRODUCTION & DEVELOPMENT began his career at Marvel Studios in 2006 as the assistant to Louis D'Esposito on *Iron Man*. Winderbaum went on to win an Emmy Award and a Webby Award in 2007 for his independently produced webseries *Satacracy 88*, then returned to Marvel to create interactive marketing campaigns for *Iron Man 2*, *Thor*, *Captain America: The First Avenger*, and *Marvel's The Avengers*. Winderbaum later went on to oversee the Marvel One-Shot program, and served as an executive producer on *Item 47*, *Agent Carter*, and *All Hail the King* before being given his first full-length project to oversee for the studio, *Ant-Man*, for which he served as co-producer. *Thor: Ragnarok* is the second feature film Winderbaum has produced for the studio.

ASSOCIATE PRODUCER BRIAN CHAPEK began his career at Marvel Studios in 2012 as a production and development assistant. Chapek went on to support the head of the Marvel One-Shots program for two installments: *Agent Carter* and *All Hail the King*. Afterward, Chapek aided in the development and production of the feature film *Ant-Man*, working directly alongside the co-producer. In 2016, before entering preproduction on *Thor: Ragnarok*, Chapek became a production and development executive for the studio.

CO-PRODUCER AND VICE PRESIDENT OF PHYSICAL PRODUCTION DAVID GRANT joined Marvel Studios in 2008. As co-producer, he recently oversaw production on *Thor: Ragnarok* and *Guardians of the Galaxy Vol. 2*, having formerly served in the same role on *Guardians of the Galaxy*, *Ant-Man*, and *Doctor Strange*. Additional credits include work as associate producer on *Iron Man 2*, *Thor*, *Marvel's The Avengers*, and *Thor: The Dark World*. Current projects include *Black Panther* and *Captain Marvel*. Prior to joining Marvel Studios, Grant was a freelance production supervisor, having worked on *Fast and Furious*, *Iron Man*, *Spider-Man 3*, *Guess Who*, and *Spider-Man 2*.

CINEMATOGRAPHER JAVIER AGUIRRESAROBE was born in Eibar, Gipuzkoa Province, Spain, in 1948. Since graduating as a director of photography from the Madrid Film School, he has participated in about 70 feature films. His awards include six Goyas (Spanish Film Academy Awards) and the 2006 National Film Award, Spain's highest honor for its industry. After 2000, Aguirresarobe's work began to be more recognized outside of Spain—including Alejandro Amenabar's *The Others* and *The Sea Inside*, Pedro Almodovar's *Talk to Her*, and Woody Allen's *Vicky Cristina Barcelona*. In the United States, Aguirresarobe shot John Hillcoat's *The Road*, which was accorded a nomination for Cinematography by the British Academy of Film and Television Arts. His recent films include *Warm Bodies* by Jonathan Levine, *Identity Thief* by Seth Gordon, *Blue Jasmine* by Woody Allen, *Goosebumps* by Rob Letterman, and *The Finest Hours* by Craig Gillespie.

PRODUCTION DESIGNER DAN HENNAH won the 2004 Academy Award (with Production Designer Grant Major) for Best Art Direction/Set Decoration on *The Lord of the Rings: The Return of the King*. He also earned several other awards and nominations for his work on the film, notably his second Art Directors Guild honor for Period or Fantasy Film. Hennah served as supervising art director and set decorator on the first three of Peter Jackson's Tolkien adaptations, working alongside designer Major and his own wife, Chris, who managed the production's Art Department. He earned Oscar nominations for his work on the first two Lord of the Rings features, *The Fellowship of the Ring* and *The Two Towers* (also winning an Art Directors Guild prize for the latter), and would reteam with Major on Jackson's 2005 reboot of *King Kong*, earning his fourth Oscar and Art Directors Guild nominations. Hennah's history with Jackson dates back to the filmmaker's 1996 horror film *The Frighteners*, on which he served as art director. When Jackson returned to the world of Tolkien with The Hobbit trilogy in 2012-14, Hennah returned as the series' production designer. He picked up his fifth Oscar nomination for the first title, *The Hobbit: An Unexpected Journey*, as well as his sixth Art Directors Guild nod. He would add yet another nomination from the ADG for *The Hobbit: The Desolation of Smaug*, along with Saturn Awards (from the Academy of Science Fiction, Fantasy and Horror Films) for the first and second Hobbit features. After toiling in the locations department on a couple of screen projects, he art directed the period miniseries *Heart of the High Country*, the 1985 Jodie Foster drama *My Letter to George*, the TV drama *The Rainbow Warrior*, and the Disney adventure *The Rescue*. Hennah earned his first production-design credit on locally filmed, Canadian-financed telefilm *Adrift*. He also worked on a number of shows for Cloud Nine Entertainment, including production designing the company's breakout hit, the dystopian adventure series *The Tribe*. Hennah most recently served as production designer for Tim Burton's *Alice Through the Looking Glass*. He also designed *Underworld: Rise of the Lycans* and the big-budget Asian Western *The Warrior's Way*, both filmed on location in his homeland.

PRODUCTION DESIGNER RA VINCENT trained with his father following art school as a scenic artist on small New Zealand film and TV projects. He went on to work as a sculptor on the Lord of the Rings trilogy, and branched out into art direction and set decoration on additional big-budget films. Vincent's work as set decorator on *The Hobbit: An Unexpected Journey* earned him an Oscar nomination in 2012. His set-decoration paintings are included in the Margaret Herrick Academy Library. Vincent's first film as production designer was Jemaine Clement and Taika Waititi's 2013 comedy *What We Do in the Shadows*. He would again work with Waititi in 2017 in *Thor: Ragnarok*, alongside longtime collaborator Dan Hennah. With his various skills, Ra involves himself in many aspects of the design process, from creating concept art to project management, set design, and set decoration. He has run projects and assembled local Art Department crews in London, Paris, Los Angeles, Toronto, Berlin, Hong Kong, and throughout Australia and New Zealand.

COSTUME DESIGNER MAYES C. RUBEO has fashioned the wardrobes for a diverse slate of movie projects in a career spanning over 25 years, including her designs for James Cameron's 2009 landmark 3-D spectacle *Avatar*, the highest-grossing film in Hollywood history. A native of Mexico City, Rubeo completed her studies in costume design at Los Angeles Trade-Technical College and earned an associate of arts degree from UCLA before studying art history at Institute Statale d'Arte in Italy. Early in her career, Rubeo collaborated with directors such as Oliver Stone (*Born on the Fourth of July*) and Paul Verhoeven (*Total Recall*). She worked with independent filmmaker John Sayles as designer on *Men with Guns*, *Sunshine State*, and *Casa De Los Babys*, and as assistant designer on *Lone Star*. In 2002, Rubeo garnered her first Costume Designers Guild Award nomination for the TV movie *Fidel*, starring Gael García Bernal. In addition to earning another CDG nomination for her work on *Avatar*, she garnered acclaim for her wardrobes on Mel Gibson's *Apocalypto*, Andrew Stanton's *John Carter*, Marc Forster's *World War Z*, James Wong's *Dragonball: Evolution*, and Duncan Jones' *Warcraft*. Before entering the Marvel Universe, Rubeo added yet another acclaimed filmmaker to her résumé: the great Chinese director Zhang Yimou, for whom she designed the ancient period costumes for his epic adventure *The Great Wall*.

PROPERTY MASTER RICHIE DEHNE is from Sydney, Australia. His background is art, rock and roll, and challenging the mainstream. He has served as property master on films around the world—contemporary, historical, fantastical, and more recently, the superhero genre. His inspiration in developing props for *Thor: Ragnarok* was helped along by the incredible art of Jack Kirby, Italian futurism, acid rock, street art, and Saturday-morning cartoons. His heroes are the artists he works with who help bring his vision to life.

VISUAL DEVELOPMENT SUPERVISOR ANDY PARK studied as an art/illustration major at both UCLA and Art Center College of Design. His career began as a comic-book artist fulfilling a childhood dream and illustrating such titles as *Tomb Raider*, *Excalibur*, and *Uncanny X-Men* for Marvel, DC, and Image Comics, among others. After a decade in the comic-book industry, he made a career switch and began working as a concept artist in video games. He was one of the leading artists designing the various worlds and fantastical characters and creatures of the award-winning *God of War* video-game franchise for Sony Computer Entertainment of America. Park joined the Visual Development Department at Marvel Studios in 2010 as a visual development concept artist, designing characters and providing keyframe illustrations for *Marvel's The Avengers*, *Iron Man 3*, *Captain America: The Winter Soldier*, *Thor: The Dark World*, *Guardians of the Galaxy*, *Avengers: Age of Ultron*, *Ant-Man*, *Captain America: Civil War*, and *Guardians of the Galaxy Vol. 2*. He has since become the visual development supervisor on *Thor: Ragnarok*, as well as the upcoming *Ant-Man & the Wasp* and *Captain Marvel*.

VISUAL EFFECTS PRODUCER CYNDI OCHS has been helping usher cutting-edge visual effects to the silver screen for the past 20 years. Ochs spent 12 years at Weta Digital in Wellington, New Zealand, where she held several roles including visual effects producer, head of production, and visual effects executive producer. During her time in New Zealand, Ochs was a leader in production organization for Academy Award-nominated films such as The Lord of the Rings trilogy, *King Kong*, *Rise of the Planet of the Apes*, *Dawn of the Planet of the Apes* and *The Jungle Book*. Ochs has also spent time on the studio side, acting as visual effects producer on *U2-3D* and *Aliens in the Attic*, and as the New Zealand on-set VFX producer for *Avatar*. This is Ochs' first film with Marvel Studios.

HEAD OF VISUAL DEVELOPMENT RYAN MEINERDING has been active as a freelance concept artist and illustrator in the film business since 2005. Even early in his career, his work was already drawing the kinds of raves reserved for industry veterans. After earning a degree in industrial design from Notre Dame, he transitioned to Hollywood and worked on 2008's *Outlander*. He was hired at Marvel Studios for *Iron Man*, and after leaving briefly to do concept work for *Transformers: Revenge of the Fallen* and *Watchmen*, has been full-time ever since. While working on *Iron Man 2*, Meinerding contributed the design for the new Iron Man armor in the comic-book series *Invincible Iron Man*. He served as visual development co-supervisor on *Captain America: The First Avenger*, *Thor*, and *Marvel's The Avengers*. He then served as head of visual development on *Iron Man 3*, *Captain America: The Winter Soldier*, *Avengers: Age of Ultron*, *Captain America: Civil War*, *Doctor Strange*, *Spider-Man: Homecoming* and the upcoming *Black Panther*. He is currently working on *Avengers: Infinity War* and loving every minute of it.

VISUAL EFFECTS SUPERVISOR AND SECOND UNIT DIRECTOR JAKE MORRISON created the visual effects for *Thor: Ragnarok*, directed by Taika Waititi. His previous work with Marvel includes 2015's big-screen hit *Ant-Man*, directed by Peyton Reed, his creations for which his creations earned a BAFTA nomination. As VFX supervisor on *Thor: The Dark World*, directed by Alan Taylor, he shared a Saturn Award nomination from the Academy of Science Fiction, Fantasy and Horror Films. He began his tenure with Marvel as second unit supervisor on Joss Whedon's *Marvel's The Avengers*. Morrison has been blending photography and computer graphics for over 25 years. Pursuing an early interest in creating real-time visuals to be performed alongside live music, Morrison taught himself a programming language and learned video-sampling techniques. Since then, he has pursued a career as a VFX/CG supervisor as well as a lead compositor on tent-pole films including Peter Jackson's Oscar-winning *The Lord of the Rings: The Two Towers* and Zac Snyder's *300*, as well as numerous commercial and television credits. Other motion-picture credits, in assorted VFX roles, include *Mission Impossible II*, *Spider-Man*, a trio of projects for the Wachowski siblings (*Speed Racer*, *The Matrix Reloaded*, and *The Matrix Revolutions*), *Charlie's Angels: Full Throttle*, and *Harry Potter and the Sorcerer's Stone*.

PARK ►

ACKNOWLEDGMENTS 2017

Anthony Allan
Victoria Alonso
Alexis Auditore
Jonay Martin
Bacallado

Mitch Bell
Laurent Ben-Mimoun
Aleksi Briclot
Nicky Campbell
Eric Hauserman

Carroll
Brian Chapek
Vince Colletta
Christian Cordella
Louis D'Esposito

Matt Delmanowski
Erika Denton
Mariano A. Diaz
Ben Donnelly
Alex Drummond

Kevin Feige
Anthony Francisco
Rodney Fuentebella
Devin Gary
David Grant

Aidan Gray
Sean Hargreaves
Todd Harris
Brendan Heffernan
Jake Hempson

Jeffrey Huet
Elissa Hunter
Ian Joyner
Andrew Kattie
Jack Kirby

Michael Kutsche
Pervical Lanuza
Dale Mackie
Dave McCaig
Randy McGowan

Daniela Medeiros
Ryan Meinerding
Till Nowak
Olyoptics 2.0
Karla Ortiz

Carlo Pagulayan
Andy Park
Avia Perez
Will Corona Pilgrim
Jacque Porte

Ryan Potter
Wil Rees
Raj Rihal
John Romita Sr.
Adam Ross

Eleni Roussos
Francisco Ruiz
Stephen Schirle
Constantine Sekeris
Emmanuel Shiu

Walter Simonson
Chris Sotomayor
Tully Summers
Jackson Sze
Ra Vincent

Taika Waititi
Brad Winderbaum
Leinil Francis Yu

■ SZE
■ 328 **RUIZ** AFTER **KIRBY**

ARTIST CREDITS

Anthony Allan
Pages 24-25, 29, 116, 244, 246-247, 277, 283, 289

Jonay Martin Bacallado
Pages 67, 73, 77, 88-89, 113, 126-128, 132, 146-147, 153, 158-163, 198, 208-209

Laurent Ben-Mimoun
Pages 16-17, 28-29, 61-63, 122-125, 138-143, 228-229, 238-239, 241, 255, 257-261

Aleksi Briclot
Pages 30-35, 38-40, 72-73, 81, 94-95, 103-104, 128-129, 155, 182-183, 197, 199, 201, 276, 278, 280, 294, 310-311, 318-319

Nicky Campbell
Pages 266-267, 289, 299

Vince Colletta
Pages 13-14

Christian Cordella
Pages 112, 164-165

Adam Del Re
Additional Design for Pages 16-17, 64-65, 122-123, 168-169, 228-229, 266-267

Mariano A. Diaz
Pages 114, 164, 188, 268-269

Ben Donnelly
Pages 250-252

Alex Drummond
Pages 166-167, 211

Anthony Francisco
Pages 23, 37, 66-71, 96, 99, 104, 113, 128, 137, 144-145, 181, 186, 192, 216-217, 274-275, 280-281, 286-287, 293

Rodney Fuentebella
Pages 196, 311

Devin Gary
Page 130

Aidan Gray
Page 249

Sean Hargreaves
Pages 157, 202-204, 245

Todd Harris
Pages 146, 220-221

Brendan Heffernan
Pages 61, 74-75, 77, 116, 125, 156-157, 171, 204-205, 237, 240, 244-245, 248, 254, 272, 288-289

Jake Hempson
Pages 30, 72, 104, 113, 117, 173, 177, 200, 212, 290, 292

Jeffrey Huet
Page 15

Ian Joyner
Pages 44-60, 62, 83-84, 100-103, 106-107, 177, 181, 186, 278

Andrew Kattie
Page 171

Jack Kirby
Pages 13-14

Michael Kutsche
Pages 42, 120-121, 154, 175, 185, 197, 279, 282-283, 306-307

Dale Mackie
Pages 159, 264-265

Dave McCaig
Page 15

Daniela Medeiros
Page 205

Ryan Meinerding
Pages 97, 133, 196, 212-215, 218-219

Till Nowak
Pages 242-244, 249, 308-309, 321

Olyoptics 2.0
Page 13

Karla Ortiz
Pages 43, 99, 136, 151-152, 180-181, 184, 197

Carlo Pagulayan
Page 15

Andy Park
Dustjacket
Pages 20-21, 80-87, 90-93, 97, 135, 137, 188-191, 193, 222-227, 245, 284-285, 296-297, 320-321, 323-325

Wil Rees
Pages 26-29, 117

Raj Rihal
Pages 130-131, 248, 256

John Romita Sr.
Page 15

Adam Ross
Page 213

Francisco Ruiz
Cover
Pages 1, 148-149, 172, 206-207, 230-235, 250, 328

Stephen Schirle
Page 144

Constantine Sekeris
Pages 132-136, 150, 152, 154, 174, 198, 290-291, 293

Emmanuel Shiu
Pages 141, 170, 283

Walter Simonson
Page 13

Chris Sotomayor
Page 15

Tully Summers
Pages 48, 52-53, 102, 105, 108-109, 144, 176-179, 181, 184, 186-187, 279, 295

Jackson Sze
Pages 3-5, 18-19, 22-23, 36, 41, 49, 76, 110-111, 118-119, 145, 153, 158, 194-195, 245, 262-263, 268, 270-271, 273, 300-305, 312-317, 326

THE THIRD FLOOR, Inc.
Pages 6-7

Ra Vincent
Pages 236-237, 253, 298

Taika Waititi
Pages 9-12

Leinil Francis Yu
Page 15

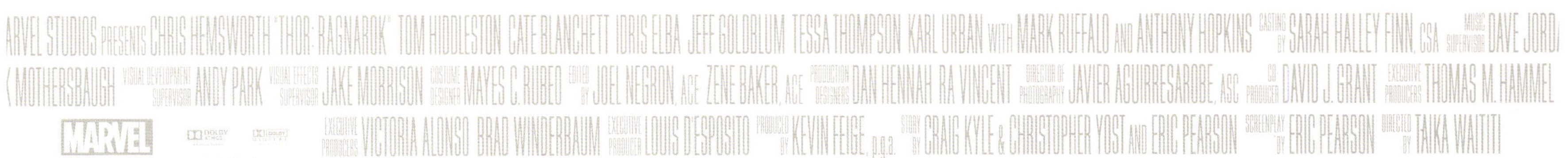